COSMIC RELIGION

a cosmocentric perspective on intelligent life

by

Thomas J. Kardos, M.S.

Order this book online at www.trafford.com
or email orders@trafford.com

Most Trafford titles are also available at major online book retailers.

Note for Librarians: A cataloguing record for this book is available from Library
and Archives Canada at www.collectionscanada.ca/amicus/index-e.html

Printed in Victoria, BC, Canada.

ISBN: 978-1-4269-1694-6 (sc)

Library of Congress Control Number: 2009935536

*Our mission is to efficiently provide the world's finest, most comprehensive book publishing
service, enabling every author to experience success. To find out how to publish your book, your
way, and have it available worldwide, visit us online at www.trafford.com*

Trafford rev. 8/31/2009

 www.trafford.com

North America & international
toll-free: 1 888 232 4444 (USA & Canada)
phone: 250 383 6864 ♦ fax: 812 355 4082

I dedicate this book to Nagy Ilona (Ica Néni) who was my 4th grade teacher in Hungary and introduced me to religion, my wife Masako who helped foster my spiritual growth with Eastern philosophies, our three wonderful children, and to the spirit of exploration in all of us.

FORWARD:

The purpose of this book is no less than to unite the world's major religions. Starting from their likely origin in human culture on this planet, we aim to take the reader through new age worldviews and pantheistic thinking to arrive at a united philosophy that is reasonable even for atheists. Bringing together the scientific, engineering, religious and historical perspectives, these writings take the insatiably curious reader to the next step in spiritual evolution, a cosmic perspective that even incorporates intelligent life beyond this planet.

At first, we get down to basics. There is only one Truth, the mental model which most accurately reflects reality. We begin first by viewing the world through our senses and the extension of those senses afforded by technology, We then reach gaps of unknowing, so we take on faith the reasonable gaps in our understanding, and we then look to our historical sages for the answers. We then get a new mental model, which may not be complete, but at least it takes us to the next level; for example we might start with the geocentric solar system, move to the heliocentric solar system, and then move to a quasi solar system. This hierarchal process may be endless, but at each stage we have sufficient knowledge to keep refining the mental model as often as necessary, and by doing so, we begin to realize that the universe is comprehensible, perhaps difficult to understand mentally but still sufficiently luminous for us to realize its wonderful potential to expand our limited perceptions.

Of course, readers will react differently to these ideas. In fact, narrow mindedness is to be expected. Consider this quote:

"The human mind treats a new idea the same way as the body treats a strange protein; it rejects it." P. B. Medawar

Some will just close their minds to new ideas by accepting colloquial aphorisms, such as, "How do I know? The Bible told me so." Others will take portions of this new knowledge and integrate them into their own teachings. Others will reject it all as outrageous and arcane yet recognize a modicum of truth, perhaps recalling Jesus' idea that "The truth will set you free." Then there are the agnostics and atheists who may not be sure of the facts but are willing to check them out at least. The author's intent is not to deflate or inflate any position but just to see how the ideas can be integrated into a mental model. We believe that the observations of scientists and the evidence of extraterrestrial life allow us to stretch our minds and perceive new meanings and values to our earthly lives. Imagine what a difference it would make if there were new sources of energy, a plethora of new scriptures, and extensive civilizations "out there" for us to meet. Think of what we could learn from cosmic history, and how it could help us avoid repeating mistakes made by other civilizations throughout the cosmos. Of course, these ideas are mind-boggling but not so abstruse nor intangible that they cannot be approached and integrated into our views about reality.

Some readers will see the light this work attempts to shine; others will react and close their minds. There are certainly enough controversial ideas presented here to stretch the limits of every sect of every religion. At the same time, we present a path that can reconcile and unite their teachings. This is a worthy goal, the achievement of which requires an open mind to see everything from a mental model of a broader perspective.

Each field of study can benefit. From the scientific perspective, it offers a measure by which a mental model is judged and how it incorporates known facts and observations yet provides a plateau for increased awareness. From a theological perspective, it offers the opportunity to include a philosophy that explains human suffering and offers miracles of regeneration usually unseen or relegated to parlor card tricks. Both the scientific view and the spiritual view can be achieved together. Overall, we present a cosmic worldview, a new paradigm, which fits our known facts and observations and which explains the healings and miracles previously held to be supernatural. After all, from a strictly biological perspective, our human existence seems like a random occurrence. Against all odds we are alive, and our self-awareness forms a vast sea of consciousness that reaches across the universe.

There are no references presented in this work other than those mentioned in the text. We ask our readers to seek out further evidence as they may require on the given material. The books, authors, subjects and referenced material discussed are easily available through simple searches of libraries, journals and the internet. No amount of evidence and proof is sufficient for the mind that is made up. Sadly, the evidence required for some who are more balanced in their reasoning may also not be available. Still, there are revelations in this volume that are likely to astound all readers.

We hope that the vast majority of our readers will benefit from this material. Most enlightened people in today's unpredictable world have seen enough in their lifetime to shock them out of narrow-mindedness. We have all experienced reversals of beliefs about one subject or another. Likewise, when we are given new facts about unusual subjects such as stem cell research, cloning, genetic therapies and the theory of relativity, they amazed us and offered us the opportunity to increase our understandings. We have all learned through our own experiences and became wiser through our own mistakes. Such learning, while disruptive, may still be sufficiently engaging to consider its possibilities. The same is true for earth-shattering discoveries. For example, should stem cell research and DNA based therapies continue to advance, the dangerous and painful surgeries of the past may seem like the activities of a backward civilization. Perhaps it would be wise to consider Schopenhauer's famous triad.

1) At first an idea is resisted.
2) Then the idea is actively opposed.
3) Finally, the idea is accepted as self-evident.

The ideas in this book probably are within stage one or two above. Still, they are worth exposing either to an open-minded world or a skeptical world.
One way to take away the emotional stigma of a new

idea finding its place is to realize that the universe is based on natural laws. They operate throughout our local environment, the larger world, and the entire cosmos. They are fair, consistent, and trustworthy, to the extent we can comprehend them. Whether expressed by the words of a priest or a biologist, a person of Eastern or Western culture, a child or a scholar, we can all agree that actions have consequences, and we exist in a universe of causes and effects. Once we examine them dispassionately, we can move forward to an increased understanding of our universe while understanding that it is constantly changing and evolving. To access these ideas is not simply to say to the world, "Look, look, look" as a child might way to an observing and admiring parent but instead to claim such ideas to enhance our lives. It gives us a reason for living that far exceeds the ordinary trends of people's limited consciousness and accesses instead -- a united cosmic spiritual understanding.

Albert Moorin, PhD

CONTENTS

Forward:		vii
Chapter 1	– The Journey Begins	1
Chapter 2	– The Truth of Life Movement: The Starting Point	9
Chapter 3	– Knowing that God Does Not Punish Man	13
Chapter 4	– What is an Alien?	20
Chapter 5	– Lord God of the Old Testament	22
Chapter 6	– Who was Jehovah? – The one portrayed as God	26
Chapter 7	– Einstein's Relativity and Religion	33
Chapter 8	– Modern Evidence of Earth Visitation and Intervention	42
Chapter 9	– Origin of Religions – from Jehovah to Christ to Muhammad – a Continuum of Guidance	48
Chapter 10	– Protecting the Earth from Man	56
Chapter 11	– Hybrid Children and the future of Homo Sapiens	59
Chapter 12	– The Future – A Cosmic Humanity	65
Chapter 13	– What Does This All Mean to Our Daily Lives?	70

Chapter 14 – Truth and Post-Traumatic
        Stress Disorder   78

Chapter 15 – Facts and Hypotheses   84

Chapter 16 – Cosmic Sutra (a summary in
        prose)   86

Chapter 17 – Cosmic Poem: Dance of the
        Black Holes   95

About the Author: 97

Chapter 1 – The Journey Begins

The world is flat. The world is round. Christ has died. Christ has risen. We make war to achieve peace. And there is sin, but it's forgiven. Such contradicting thoughts fly through my mind as a strong northerly wind fills my sails on my way down the Mexican coastline, just south of San Diego, to who-knows-where. It's the late autumn of 2004, and there is no other vessel or human being in sight. I am flying along at over ten knots in my little trimaran named Therapy, a name that suggests calmness and restoration to health. At this time it was more of an irony since the weather was severe enough for the Coast Guard to issue a small craft warning of bad weather. As if in anticipation of my thoughts, just then a big red helicopter flies up from behind me and hovers a few hundred feet high with big letters on the side unmistakably spelling the words US COAST GUARD. But I have no fear, not of the weather nor of the big ship up above. Slowly, I wave toward its pilot, with the unspoken message, "Thank you for your concern, but I'm fine." The craft hovers for a while, so I wave again. Then, as if understanding, it turns and flies to the north toward my adopted country, the USA, which I will not see again for several months. I am on a trek and not to be dissuaded. I have a purpose and a goal both for my outward journey toward an unknown destination and for my inner journey which is my quest for Truth. Although such an inner or outer journey seems senseless to the logical mind, for me it is quite tangible, a kind of inchoate creative process bound to achieve its mark. I will not rest until I achieve it!

My sailboat, thirty-five feet long and eighteen feet wide, consisted of three hulls – a main center hull and two outer hulls like those of a catamaran, all connected together in triplicate, which is why it is called a trimaran. Although the craft is small and at times topsy-turvy, it is, in fact, both stable and safe since damage to any one hull will still allow it to stay upright and sail to safety using the other two.

My history with the trimaran corroborated its sturdiness and reliability. When I sailed from Los Angeles to Hawaii a few years earlier in 2001, I had a problem. The rudder broke and sank about two-thirds of the way there or 1600 miles out from L.A. and about 800 miles from Hilo. This little disaster may have been expected since the date was September 11, 2001, a day of bad luck for too many people. At the time I had not heard of the attack. When I did hear about it several days later, like many people I was shocked. It just shows how alone one can be out at sea without the ordinary contacts with civilization. It was like being on another world.

To make matters worse, although I had several global position satellite receivers for navigation, my rudder was gone, so I was at the mercy of the winds and could not trim the sails for a few days. Then I figured out a way to steer by dragging a ripped sail from the backside of either the right or the left hull. Since a trimaran is relatively wide, this selective drag provided a measure of control, although it also slowed the boat down to just a few knots.

Eventually, I made it to Hilo, Hawaii, after a month alone out at sea, a 2400 mile trip. My wife came out to visit for a few days. Then I sailed across the islands for a month, sold my boat, and flew home.

Three years later, during my present trip, I ended up 3022 miles from San Pedro and the Los Angeles Harbor. My original destination was Costa Rica; however, on account of an old one-dollar chart of the Galapagos archipelago that I purchased on a whim just before leaving, I ended up plotting a course out there from the southernmost port of Golfito in Costa Rica and eventually ended up crossing the equator for the first time in my life (see the picture on the back cover). This apparently wayward journey, however, was necessary. I recall Edward Albee's famous quote: "Sometimes it's necessary to go a long distance out of the way in order to come back a short distance correctly."

This quote turned out to be a self-fulfilling prophecy. This trip enabled me to encounter different cultures and countries and fine-tune my navigating skills. It was also nearly twice as long in time and challenged me to manage the occasional minor disaster that befell my boat and the emotional ups and downs and loneliness that engulfed my mind, something that happens to every explorer or sailor. What had previously been merely charts and maps and mere names, for me became an adventure in curiosity.

My subconscious mind roamed freely and guided me to unearth ideas about our existence on the planet as part of a vast unknown universe, and my conscious mind fed me ideas to keep me safe. Overall, it was a harmonious mixture of my sixth sense and my thinking processes. My insatiable curiosity was the moving force, the juggernaut that enabled me to feel invincible as a Marco Polo yet also as vulnerable as a child. All in all, I did not experience the distractions from everyday living with its casual conversations and shallow concerns. During my Hawaiian trip I learned to listen and learn from my inner voice. This is not religious nor mystical nor biological; it is what we all have if we are willing to find it within ourselves through the process of relaxation and inner quiet. I learned to trust this inner guidance, which made me feel less afraid of being alone as I headed toward the unknown. This pattern represented my inner journey, which impelled me always to go forward, the same philosophical message of General Patton during World War II as he achieved victory after victory. Going forward, always going forward, whether fast or slow, was most important.

To the logical mind, this inner mantra could just as easily refer to pigs going through a chute, ultimately to be slaughtered. But for me, going forward had an inner, directed quest. It is based on a hybrid Buddhist / Christian teaching which states that we are all Children of God, that we have inherited the power to create and change the world, and that the concept of sin is a delusion. By seeking our inner God-nature and acting in accordance with it, we cannot go wrong and commit what the Judeo-Christian religion would call sin. Furthermore, according to this teaching, the true omnipresent God does not punish people nor allow anything or anyone to get sick or be imperfect. Sickness or suffering is an illusion, and our true nature and true image is that of a perfect being. After all, God is perfect; how could He create imperfection? The laws of the universe – though we may not fully understand them – are unchanging and perfect. Each of us is a small universe, a perfect and harmonious assemblage of its components down to each subatomic particle, and in a sense with God residing within. When we have explored our tremendous inner resources, we can expect not only the spiritual gifts of prophesy, mind travel, and immunity from danger but also the material gifts – excellent health, supportive friends, career success, and enough supply to spare and share.

I believe this concept of spirituality gives me comfort and confidence to undertake my so-called perilous journey. I also believe that if people would subscribe to this concept, then they could find peace on Earth, alleviate fear and suffering, and live in joy and harmony.

The only problem is – many cannot do it. They do not have the discipline to act according to their best judgment and rely on their inner subconscious guide. Our world is usually too noisy to hear the subconscious voice, let alone try to follow it. Many people react instead of proact, and in both cases tend to act selfishly instead of altruistically. Why? Because they cannot feel each other's pain and suffering or joy and pleasure. If they could sense such emotions from one another and actually feel them within themselves, then they would naturally act more harmoniously.

Consider this hypothetical situation: If I could feel your pain in my mind, would I want to kick you? If I could sense your pain the moment you sense it yourself, would I want to hurt you even more so? On a more global scale, if I could sense everybody's pain, would I want to hurt anyone? – or would I try to prevent everyone from being hurt? The answers to these questions are no, no, no! If I could feel the pain of others, I would not hurt them since I do not want them to feel pain just as I would not want to feel pain.

By contrast, if I could feel the joy and pleasure of others in my mind as if they were my own, then I would proactively try to cause joy and pleasure to all others so that I could benefit from feeling this positive emotion myself. We want to feel joy and pleasure ourselves, so we cause others to feel this way and thus feel the boomerang effect on ourselves.

In a sense this concept when acted upon creates telepathy between people, all of whom are benefiting others as they benefit themselves. Just like the waves of the sea lead to other waves, together they help the whole ocean; it's synergistic, that is the whole then becomes greater than the individual parts, a universal harmony.

Here is a simple everyday example to illustrate both sides of the equation. Suppose there are ten boys, and one of them is given ten candy bars. Would he tend to distribute one each to the others or try to eat all ten himself? Well, if he can only feel his own hunger and sense of taste, he would eat as many as he can himself and then distribute the rest to the others, which from a higher perspective would appear to be gluttonous and selfish. However, if he could feel the hunger of the others, he would share the candy bars right away and feel the happiness of the others, which, of course, would come back to him. This example identifies the value of our sixth sense. When we feel in our own minds what others feel, then we would naturally behave in ways that would bring the greatest good to everyone else as well.

Thinking of everyone else as well as ourselves is not simply being generous; it is the way human beings function best because from the perspective of sociology, physics and other natural principles, they are all linked. So what hurts one hurts all and what benefits one, if shared, benefits all.

It has an even broader context. Just as the ecosystems are interdependent so are the needs of human beings. Furthermore, human beings are connected with the ecosystem, so if humans benefit the ecosystem, the ecosystem benefits them.

It all sounds so simple, yet the world is seemingly so complex. We might legitimately ask about the links that trigger an earthquake or tsunami or wave of prosperity. Whether it is a link to the earth's tectonic plates or the world's money system, its relevance exists everywhere on the planet. Even in these situations there is a connection between loved ones.

We have all heard of or experienced ourselves some instances where strong emotions such as those caused by terror or trauma of a family member or close friend is suddenly felt across many miles and is confirmed afterwards by a phone call or other conventional message. It has unmistakably happened in my family, but is hard to study scientifically due to the apparent rarity of such events and the difficulty in creating the circumstances and effects in a controlled laboratory environment.

Still, the recognition of such subliminal communication demonstrates that human beings and other species are interconnected, and particle physics and the study of electromagnetism with its sophisticated technology has shown this connection and nearly proven its existence.

In a way, this idea has two opposite sides: it can make a human being into a monsters or a saint. Human beings acting as Frankensteins have the capacity and sometimes unfortunately the will power to blow up the world. But even the fictional Frankenstein matures and realizes that men should not be alone and, in fact, need one another. Even monstrous people need to accept and give and receive love, not hurt themselves and others. So, in any sense of the word, atomic weapons are obviously unthinkable because they hurt everyone and everything. The only idealistic, ethical, and harmonious choice is to relinquish such weaponry and embark upon an inner journey that realizes the harmony of everything. This idea suggests that human beings should be saints. I think they can be.

In a world with over six billion people on earth and many billions of life forms elsewhere in an endless and breathtaking universe, there needs to be a concerted effort to move into this next major paradigm. To make this idea become real, humans do have to become more saint-like. Such an idea is certainly possible. In presenting my ideas, that is my outward and inward journey, I will demonstrate that it is not just possible but mandatory.

CHAPTER 2 – THE TRUTH OF LIFE MOVEMENT: THE STARTING POINT

During my previous solo trip to Hawaii in 2001, I read extensively from the teachings of *Seicho No Ie*, a Japanese religious philosophy founded in 1930 by Dr. Masaharu Taniguchi. This movement later spread to other countries, notably to Brazil and the United States, its main center being in Gardena, California. The English name for the movement is Truth of Life or the International Peace-by-Faith Movement. This is a hybrid Buddhist and Christian teaching which espouses three main principles:

1) We are all children of God.
2) Sickness is a delusion.
3) Sin too is a delusion.

It also teaches that Jesus Christ was not the only son or child of God, but instead emphasizes this famous Biblical quote: "Ye are gods; and all of you are children of the Most High" (*Psalms 82:6*, and quoted in *John 10:34*). Consequently, we all have the power of God to create and to heal. We too can heal sickness as Jesus did; however, he was more in tune with his God-nature within him than the rest of us and therefore could do it more easily. *Seicho No Ie* also teaches that God does not judge and deal out punishment since there is no sin to punish. We are responsible for judging and punishing ourselves. Notice that this idea alone – that we are not sinners but children of God – eliminates the collective guilt that has permeated our world for centuries.

Notice too that the removal of this guilt can give human beings the opportunity to explore their potentials.

Although such ideas are contrary to conventional teachings, its proponents, nonetheless, do not indulge in disputes or conflicts with other teachings but instead wish to see the good in all teachings. Such hybrid teachings, such as Seicho No Ie, are very helpful in bringing people of different religions together, especially since religious differences have themselves been the cause of many wars and much suffering throughout human history.

At first glance, however, there are still apparent contradictions with scientific discoveries. For example, if we look at Albert Einstein's theory of relativity, whether correct of not, it can explain all observed phenomena and promote a universal and consistent body of thought. If a religious philosophy or concept, such as *Seicho No Ie*, could encompass most of the ideas of scripture, unite with other spiritual teachings and rationally explain the recorded events in those scriptures, then it would be possible to demonstrate reasons for some agreement between religion and science.

The key to this mutual understanding is looking at both from a higher perspective. Consider Albert Einstein's way of pointing to this perspective. When he was faced with the apparent contradictions of measuring the speed of light from different perspectives and frames of reference, he postulated a simple and elegant rule that made perfect sense, no matter how strange the results. He said that the speed of light is constant in any frame of reference, even if one frame is in motion relative to the other. Thus if follows that time itself must change in one frame of reference compared to the other – which is a difficult deduction, but must be true if the original postulation about the speed of light is correct. From this reasoning, he also claimed additional deductions such as the "twin paradox," where one twin is accelerated away from the other twin in a ship close to the speed of light, then later stops and returns. The twin who stayed behind will have aged more than the twin that was accelerated close to the speed of light because his time as well as all clocks that travel with him "paradoxically" slows down during the journey. This result is part of the Special Theory of Relativity, which dates back to 1905, and has been confirmed experimentally over the past 100+ years.

This higher perspective demonstrates a simple and elegant starting point that would help resolve the fundamental difference between science and religion.

This simple starting point is the pantheistic view that God is omnipresent within the Universe, perfect and harmonious, and, as Seicho No Ie teaches, God does not punish man. In other words, God is not a person who plays favorites of one person over another but rather exists everywhere. Consequently, His mind may be understood by studying and comprehending the underlying rational principles upon which the world functions. From this starting point, the first major contradiction and question would be this: If God does not punish man, who is responsible for the repeated biblical descriptions of punishments in the Book of Genesis and elsewhere? We will pursue this line of reasoning in the following chapter.

CHAPTER 3 – KNOWING THAT GOD DOES NOT PUNISH MAN

A while back, I had a conversation with a Jewish friend of mine about the Seicho-No-Ie teachings, who was at a particularly difficult time of his life. I suggested to him that God does not punish us, does not judge us, and that only man judges and punishes other men, so there is no need to fear God. With a slight chuckle indicating his mild disbelief, he replied: "what about the Egyptians, and what about Sodom and Gomorrah?" Of course, he was referring to the Biblical stories in the Old Testament (Book of Genesis), where Moses led his people out of bondage by the help of God, who punished the Egyptians; and about the two ancient cities that were destroyed by God as punishment for their deviant ways. We all saw Charlton Heston in the Cecil B. DeMille classic of The Ten Commandments. In the movie as in the Bible, the Jewish Exodus was preceded by increasingly harsh acts of punishment from God upon the Egyptian people, each one followed by a cry from Moses: "Let my people go!" Did God actually punish the Egyptian people? Did God punish the people of Sodom and Gomorrah? Does God punish people today, and should we fear Him?

If one rises to a higher level of consciousness and looks at these events from the perspective of an expanded worldview, the truth becomes clear that God did not punish anyone. The need to fear God has been inspired by major religions because it was useful. A Catholic priest once told me that without a fear of God, most people would feel free to commit horrendous acts of crime otherwise. So what explanation can there be for the apparent actions that have been attributed to God in the holy scriptures? How can these Biblical stories and the current belief culture be reconciled with the teaching that we are all children of God, perfect and harmonious, and need not fear God's punishments for sinful acts, since God does not judge man?

If we meditate and contemplate upon such questions, and bring into consideration the lessons of an increasingly large number of modern day witnesses to extraordinary events and allow our worldview to expand without the inhibitions of our ingrained belief culture, the answers become clear, and like the pieces of a puzzle, a new worldview emerges. The first question on this new road of contemplation would be: If God did not punish the people described in these holy scriptures, then who did? – and why? Well, since we are all children of God, we too have a mind with the power to create, and we can place ourselves into God's shoes. We can contemplate what our actions would be if we were able to exist as a great expanded self, with great wisdom, power and love toward all life, able to comprehend the vast abundance in the universe, and feel joy at the magnificent harmony that synchronizes all that exists. We could place ourselves into a watchful outpost beyond the physical or mental reach of a primitive and evolving people on a special blue planet, and with our grand love, kindness and understanding, ask how we could guide these fledgling human beings toward their greater potential. How do we teach them and keep them from physical harm without taking away their inalienable rights of self-determination and freedom while nurturing the growth and development of the species? Life is special; it transforms chaos into order in spite of the second law of thermodynamics, which states that all spontaneous process result in an increase is entropy, or lead to chaos. The greater the complexity that a life-form can attain, the greater its mind, the greater its ability to create, and the closer it will come to resemble its all-powerful omnipresent Father. Taking this expression to its limit, as one does in the mathematics of calculus, given infinite time, this evolving life form will approach and attain its true and highest potential, and as its intelligence and creative ability becomes infinite, it shall be indistinguishable from God.

Life that has come to appreciate the attributes of God protects other life. Higher level life forms strive to protect lower level life forms, especially those that are most similar and approaching their own form and image. This is self-evident. If, while we are in our watchful outpost, we notice that our primitive evolving friends on that special blue planet below are attaining levels of power that may be self-destructive and cause their extinction, we feel sorrow for the potential loss of this grand life, and for the loss of the potential which they may attain. We would therefore interfere without appearing to interfere. We would impede the destructive forces, and foster the progressive ones. We would impede the destructive ways of the Egyptians, impede the unnatural ways of decadent people, and foster the behavior in the rest in a manner that promotes continued progress toward the growth and development of the rest of the species. We would suggest and promote rules of conduct that would guide the people away from widespread harm. We would pass down a simple set of commandments and impress them that following these rules will bring them benefits, and instill fear in them that avoiding these rules would bring them punishment. As long as these measures work, we would sit back and watch them carefully; and when the effectiveness of these measures wean, we would initiate other events. To disguise our actions so that we may remain undetected and continue our work, we would form our intervention to appear to be effects of the Almighty. But we would continue to act with grand love and compassion, whenever possible, as the God-nature in us dictates, as if our actions were what God would want.

Then one day, we would see a need to go beyond simple commandments and fearsome demonstrations of punishment; we would enact one of our greatest acts of love that is most personable to our evolving friends. We would communicate with selected members down there who are good communicators in themselves and inspire discussion of the impending arrival of a Great Teacher, who would be anticipated by a growing number of the people. We would communicate through these selected prophets the signs of how the arrival of this Great Teacher may be recognized, and attempt to create a receptive atmosphere so that when He does come, his message and guidance would not be rejected but would be accepted by as many of the people as possible. And after he is born, we must protect him, teach him what he needs to know, and guide him to communicate to as many people as possible a way of life and behavior that simple commandments could not do, as evidenced by the fact that our chosen nation in their promised land has forsaken our guidance over and over. We must help this Great Teacher impress his fellow men to win their attention and respect with love and compassion rather than fear and punishment, and enable Him to improve the quality of life of those who are ill and suffering as a means to invite as many of the people as possible over to His teachings, for through these teachings the probability of long term survival and growth of the species is greater than without them.

We would sadly know, however, that this effort of education will take time, and that our Teacher would be overcome on the short term with reactionary forces and people who have increasingly avoided the guidance of our previous commandments. But alas, this reactionary force will cause the very event that will result in the greatest impression upon the people – the event that will propel a great number of descendents of the existing generation to learn His teachings. In this event, we must show that someone who teaches love and kindness cannot die at the hands of those who have weaned away from our prior commandments. Though even He will not be aware of our true selves and methods, and regrettably, he will feel suffering in the process of his final actions amongst the people before we can recover him, resuscitate him, and return him to his followers for his final parting actions. Throughout his suffering in this process, even He will briefly disbelieve that a higher power is watching over him, but afterwards he will understand that it was necessary to impress the people that His teachings are of the greatest value. We must then gently lift him out in view of His faithful witnesses who will propagate his teachings into the future.

We will then again retreat to our observation post beyond detection until the need arises for another intervention. There will come a time, however, when the anticipated healthy growth and development of this species of life on the blue planet will reach a level where it will understand more and more about all that exists around them, and we will become more and more vulnerable to detection. They will naturally develop means and methods to go faster, see farther and live longer, when our old methods will become suspiciously recognizable to some of them as other than acts of the Almighty, but our own acts, even though they were acts of intervention meant to be useful and protective of their life on the planet. Some of them will witness our ongoing operations in spite of our attempts to stay secretly beyond their detection and perception. Others will realize the similarities between their own acquired technical capabilities and ours. Others yet will recognize our interventions going back in time, and realize the similarities of our methods witnessed and recorded in their holy scriptures with those witnessed today. Some of them will attempt to duplicate our means and abilities, unbeknownst to the rest, and attempt to use it to win conflicts. But hopefully, there will be some who will make the mental leap to understand that our actions were meant to protect them, throughout the growth and development of their own grand life, in the process of attaining ever-higher mental and spiritual levels and greater creative powers and toward finding their own true image and potential.

Some of them will realize that they are not the highest physical form of life, and respect and appreciate us for our help throughout their antiquity. And hopefully, some of them will realize that it was necessary to disguise our actions as those of God to stay undetected, and that any suffering we caused to some were necessary for the preservation of their life as a species. They will realize that the actual God the omnipresent has no such a persona as to reward or punish any living being, and therefore no need to be feared. They will realize that only man judges another man, and only living beings punish each another. We were acting within our own God-nature to foster and nurture their species, and in that process, it was we that selectively doled out punishment in the process of guiding the remaining people forward toward attaining their potential as a unified species on their rare and precious blue planet. And when they realize this, we hope that they will return the favor and guide other lesser forms of life toward their greater potential, and after that, we hope that we can all form a great friendship of grand intelligence.

CHAPTER 4 – WHAT IS AN ALIEN?

My wife is a resident alien. When I told my kids that their mom is an alien, they stood in disbelief. When I proved it by showing them her resident alien registration card, otherwise known as a green card, they chuckled that their definition of an alien was different – more guided by science fiction movies. Well what is the definition of an alien? Is it an extraterrestrial biological entity? Is it a life form other than ours? Is it life that evolved on a planet other than our own? Is it life that evolved at the bottom of the ocean around hot volcanic vents? The commonplace answer would be "all of the above". However, consider the fact that the principles of mathematics, physics and biochemistry are the same throughout the Universe. Einstein's theories of special and general relativity are valid everywhere. When Neil Armstrong left Earth, arrived on the Moon, and then returned, he was still the same old Neil Armstrong. He was not an alien. Likewise, men who would be physically just like us, but would have come from elsewhere in the cosmos, would also not be alien. And since all of existence is united as a whole by our common underlying building blocks, and functions similarly from one corner of the universe to the other as described by rational scientific principles, no life is truly alien. Our understanding of the world has not attained that most high level, where we comprehend all there is to know. Therefore, some forms of life out there may be different, but I would argue still not alien. As long as such life forms, though unfamiliar to most of us, are based on an expanded understanding of biochemistry, they are not alien, but rather simply our brothers and sisters or perhaps distant cousins in a grand cosmic family.

Chapter 5 – Lord God of the Old Testament

In bringing out the ideas in Chapter 5 and 6, I have discovered ambivalence in my own point of view, which parallels a dichotomy in the views of others. Although I am critical of Jehovah as he is portrayed in the Bible, I do not oppose the contents of the Bible *per se*. There are so many beautiful, inspiring passages from the books of wisdom and poetry that have stirred people's consciousness for centuries.

The stories of the Bible demonstrate religious myth at its finest. Who has not been afflicted with a Goliath-type problem that was reduced down to size thanks to the believer's use of subtle mental strategies rather than the brute force that brings the residual effects of retaliation regardless of the faults of the oppressor? Likewise, the passages from the Book of Job demonstrate the need for restraint in the midst of nagging frustrations and tragedy which seem to come from nowhere. Overall, the Bible is a compilation of stories and passages that can inspire one to overcome life's challenges.

Recognizing the inspiring features of the Bible can also help us respect the teachers and teachings based on the Bible, however different they may be from our own views. As we have established in the preceding chapters, the basis or spiritual evolution is mutual respect of our own teachings as well as those of others. Established from our birth, family, and cultural traditions, one's teaching represents the *raison d'être* for one's existence. I recall a common expression about one's favorite religion couched in these terms: once a Jew always a Jew, once a Catholic always a Catholic, and once a Mormon always a Mormon. It is a concept as profound and prevalent as one's DNA and has even morphed into the idea that "My religion is the one true religion," suggesting that the others are journeys that lead nowhere and should be avoided. Although this is an elitist, egotistical idea, it is what some people need to assure themselves that they are on the right spiritual path. Also, the idea of pluralism, choosing the best two or three teachings from several teachings, seems unfocused and off course almost as much as the stand of the agnostic, who does not know, or the atheist, who rejects all spiritual teachings. Some teachings appear to be downright contradictory. Still, people are free to worship as they choose.

Whatever differences we may have, we still owe our fellow humans the respect and gratitude of their belief system. Instead of frenetic, hair-splitting disputes about this idea or another idea, why not just accept them as others' point of view, and better yet, learn from them. The teaching of the "Tao-te-Ching" by Lao Tzu, for example, advocates eliminating all but essential possessions to focus more precisely on the spiritual path. Likewise, Jesus says to the rich man, "*Sell all thou hast, and give to the poor,*" probably an overstatement, but the point of both passages is the same: do not dwell too much on material concerns, which in the long run, will be contradictory to one's path and may indeed retard it.

So, as we look at the Old Testament, we can learn from individual passages and stories and appreciate their wisdom as a first step in respecting the Judaic-Christian point of view. Certainly, the mystical wisdom and poetry books of Psalms, Proverbs, and Isaiah can provide solace for many people. Some people love the 23rd Psalm and repeat it every morning as part of spiritual practices, and sense the wisdom and beauty of its words. Likewise, the refusal of Shadrach, Meshach, and Abednego on pain of death to reject the unjust laws of Nebuchadnezzar is a tribute to the non-violent movement for racial equality in the 1960s. Jewish families gather at home to repeat inspiring passages from the Torah to clear their minds. Likewise, attending Catholic Church, there is the value of confession to clear the soul of its emotional stresses. For Buddhists, meditation brings mental tranquility.

So, we can understand that one's spiritual practices, regardless of their origins, can make a difference in people's lives. Many agnostics and atheists as well have their reasons for their rejections of standard religious teachings, but shed light on the truth as they see it. I recall seeing a British atheist who had written a best-selling book rejecting religion, was patient and respectful of others' teachings. While one can find fault with anyone's point of view, the underlying element of respect for differences is the first step to discovering the truth. This position is obviously antithetical to the tribal mentality of religious warfare and inquisitions. Our "friends" likely agree.

So, as I mentioned before, one part of my ambivalence is a recognition of the value of the Bible and its pivotal role in articulating other points of view. Still the behavior of Jehovah known as Lord God of the Old Testament is bewildering, contradictory, mercurial, and cruel. Most believers of a god that is omniscient, omnipotent, and beneficent, would find that the Lord God figure of religious myth falls short of this idea by a landslide. In fact, as a god who played chess with the fate of the Jewish people, he matches the cliché-like idea that absolute power corrupts absolutely. So with this preface to the paradoxically divergent aspects of Jehovah, let us explore other possibilities that may make sense from another perspective.

Chapter 6 – Who was Jehovah? –
The one portrayed as God

As I was sailing down the Mexican coastline during late 2004 and early 2005, on the way to Costa Rica, I was methodically reading and studying the Old Testament, making mental notes of all the situations where there were direct interactions with Jehovah. There are numerous examples of well-documented actions that illustrate his attributes, aside from claming to be a god-like figure. Jehovah certainly had well-meaning intentions for those he considered worthy. After establishing that Abraham was one such worthy person, who was obedient and who behaved in an exemplary fashion with superlative moral character, according to Genesis 13:15, Jehovah promised him a vast land. Then in Genesis 17:2 Jehovah promised that he would make Israel into a mighty nation with millions of descendants, and later in Genesis 35:10 renamed Abraham's grandson Jacob as Israel. He had twelve sons whose descendents indeed became the twelve tribes of Israel. One of them, Joseph, was taken to Egypt, which was the beginning of the Hebrew stay in Egypt that ended four hundred years later with the Exodus led by Moses, back to the land promised to Abraham and his descendents.

Jehovah's devotion to the Israelite people started with his agreement and covenant with Abraham, which included circumcision for all descendent males (Genesis 17:10), which we now know had good scientific basis given the cleanliness of those days. So far so good.

However, this same benevolent deity changed over time, and to keep to his word and continue to guide and foster this chosen people, he performed some rather cruel actions. Why, for example, did he allow the Hebrews enslaved under the Egyptians for over 400 years if they were his favorites. Why not help them much sooner? Is he a sadistic deity that enjoys making people suffer for centuries before rescuing them? Then there is the well-known intervention to help Moses convince the Pharaoh to let the Israelites leave Egypt. The final of these interventions indirectly caused the death of all first born of the Egyptians and some of their livestock to die (Exodus 11:5), certainly not a benevolent result. This event eventually precipitated the departure of the Israelites from Egypt and is now celebrated as Passover.

There are, however, other questionable acts of Jehovah or Lord God which seem unfair and even cruel whether they are pre-meditated or not. Here are a few of them. An omnipresent and benevolent God would not perpetrate such cruel acts such as killing all of the people of Sodom, including young children and babies. What did they do to deserve divine wrath?

This behavior reminds me of a master who plays favorites with his pets at the detriment of others, to the extreme of allowing and helping his pets kill other animals for sport. At the same time, he may be angry with his pets when they do not perform up to his expectations, such as when a dog does not sit or roll over on command. Then he kills his own pets! The kind of anger displayed by Jehovah when he was ready to destroy his people for abandoning him and worshipping other Gods, then changing his mind after Moses falls to his knees and pleads on behalf of the Israelites, is indicative more of a being prone to emotional outbursts than an all-knowing benevolent and omnipresent deity. In the Book of Job, Job suffers for no apparent reason or a flimsy one at that, namely to be the fall guy of a bet between Lord God and Satan. In the process of Job learning to withstand incredible adversities, three of his wives and their children are destroyed. Why? In fact, why must innocent people be destroyed because others make mistakes.

One can make excuses for Lord God by saying that humans should never question the word of God. One should merely obey without question. For those who just follow the flow of conditioned behavior like pigs going through a chute to be destroyed, this answer is sufficient. But for those who hunger for justice and goodness, this answer is woefully inadequate and may explain rather trenchantly why people turn to atheism. Ask those whose children died in warfare or who were gassed by a malevolent enemy that this was God's Will, and the reader will understand why the World War II writer Victor Frankl, the author of *Man's Search for Meaning*, hypothetically put God on trial, along with his fellow sufferers and found God guilty. Frankly, there have been many holocausts in the world's history, and none of them needed to happen to justify the unknown motives of a so-called just god.

So, apparently there is a gap in our understanding of this so-called human god. This gap is the missing link in the question of why bad things happen to good people. Suppose this Lord God figure, as he is he pejoratively names, is not a god at all but a super being posing as God, or even an extraterrestrial who helps people as he sees fit and also destroys them as he sees fit. Follow the reasoning in the next passages carefully and decide for yourself.

Jehovah could get away with masquerading as God because of the arsenal of technology which he had at his disposal, along with a more advanced bioform which included two powers that most Homo sapiens do not have: telepathic abilities and relatively long life spans. The first of these enables them to sense mental expressions and emotions of others at a distance. Such telepathic abilities are occasionally observed in our own cultures, typically between family members or close friends during traumatic events when strong emotional states are generated. Some scientists have described thinking and the recall of memory as wave patterns upon the surface layer of the brain comprising the cortex (see Michael Talbot's *The Holographic Universe*). These surface waves are electromagnetic in nature like the electroencephalogram and would generate a stronger signal during strong emotional states. Thoughts would represent weaker signals, which only a more highly evolved brain coupled with a more highly evolved electromagnetic sensory organ can sense clearly.

The act of prayer or meditation helps with such communications, since it creates a mental state in which thoughts are organized and often sub-vocalized while the body is physically at rest. Prayer is a form of communication; however, the receiving audience may be other than who we expect. Prayers meant for one person or group can often positively influence another group. For example, people meditating outside of a Washington building during the 1970s changed the strife-ridden vibrations within the building. The other beneficial receiver was the city of Washington DC, an ordinarily crime ridden city. During the meditation of this group, however, criminal activity was measurably reduced. The second trait, a relatively long life span, is important for keeping a common and consistent agenda across numerous human generations. Even so, there must be a team of colleagues with a rotating membership over time to carry on the work since any one being would have a finite lifetime, however long that might be.

Those familiar with the concept that the technology of the future appears as the magic of today would know that phenomenal effects can be generated which appear to be so unnatural that they may be attributed to God. We already have the biotechnology and medical resuscitation procedures to enact the recorded events that comprise the resurrection and will thereafter recognize it as attributable to technology rather than an act of God.

The meaning and importance of that event is nevertheless not to be underestimated or marginalized. It is still a holy event because our guides and chess masters deemed it necessary for our cultural advancement and social survival. The manner in which Jesus Christ was raised by what appeared to be a beam of light has been observed in modern days as the method of lifting human beings who are the subjects of certain medical experiments – otherwise known as abductees. And He was not the only one observed to experience such levitation. There are descriptions in the Old Testament of angels in white robes who were otherwise normally appearing human beings, but at the end of conversation with a prophet or other selected individuals, were lifted into the air. It is this manner of transport that caused medieval and even modern painters to ascribe wings to angels, for it was their ability to lift up and apparently fly that made them physically unique.

Jehovah and his assistants who appeared to the Israelites as angels are similar to today's UFO occupants who often accompany abductees in a vertical light beam while they are ascending from their home to a space ship and then have medical procedures including artificial insemination that are not unlike the events of the immaculate conception.

To make such a correlation would not have been possible even a few decades ago. It is only today that we have within our own scientific abilities of biotechnology and within our own knowledgebase of ufology that we can connect the dots and see who and what Jehovah really must have been. He and his team represent a necessary intervention in the human culture of those days, which was occasionally cruel but overall beneficial and operated under the aura of the all-powerful god, that is different from our present enlightened view of a universal or cosmic conception of God.

Once we put Jehovah in this context, then his apparently confusing behavior as an extraterrestrial makes sense. He is not God because he does not behave as God should behave in a benevolent universe. If he is a function of an advanced technological civilization, then we can legitimately question his motives and his behavior while still appreciating the idea that subliminally we are all inherently perfect creations despite our mistakes and can still evolve to make that perfection more consistent. But let us all be careful of whom we call God. It might just be an extraterrestrial with a technological advantage. This is not the science fiction of bygone eras but the science of reality with a spiritual foundation that represents our twenty-first century!

CHAPTER 7 – EINSTEIN'S RELATIVITY
AND RELIGION

One reason that many people do not believe in long distance space travel or that visitors could have come here from another star system is because the common misconception that it would take far longer than a lifetime. Einstein was well known for his Theory of Relativity, and not so well known for his Theory of Religion; we shall examine both of these in this chapter. His theory of Special Relativity, which was published over one-hundred years ago in 1905, proposed the concept of 'time dilation', which has since been proven as a physical fact through measurements in cyclotrons. This concept is simple, and was easily understood by most freshman physics students. It states that as one travels closer to the speed of light, their time and clocks in their frame of reference slows down relative to time and clocks in the frame of reference of their origin. It also states that as one gets closer to the speed of light, his mass or weight increases, and it takes increasingly more energy to push towards higher speeds. As one approaches the speed of light from any frame of reference and measurement, an object's mass approaches infinity. In other words, it would take infinite energy to push the mass of that object all the way to 100% of the speed of light. Also, the time and clocks of the occupants would approach zero progression, and actually stop at 100% of the speed of light. In other words, we cannot travel to 100% of the speed of light, but could travel to 99.999999999% of this speed, given enough energy to accelerate us to that speed. As we approach such speeds, our internal clocks and the progression of time and aging relative to time at our origin would also slow, as illustrated by Einstein's 'twin paradox'. The key here is that we can travel great distances with little aging or apparent elapsed time in our frame of reference if we were the travelers, and able to traverse great spans of the cosmos while aging mere days or weeks. The basic formula for time dilation and mass increase is given below.

Simply said, as the speed 'v' increases to the speed of light 'c', the ratio of v/c becomes 1, and the denominator becomes zero, making the expression go to infinity. By applying this formula with increasing speeds approaching that of light, the distance traveled by a craft and the time elapsed within the craft as experienced by the traveler can be summarized by the following table:

Table 1: Special Relativity – Time Dilation

Duration of trip from the traveler's perspective (in years) using the formula:

$$\gamma = \frac{1}{\sqrt{1 - v^2/c^2}}$$

v = velocity, or speed in a straight line, c = speed of light
γ = time dilation factor, as v $\rightarrow$ c, the dilation factor approaches infinity
Duration of trip, t = (distance / γ) / speed
Note: at slow speeds, t ~ distance / speed, and as v $\rightarrow$ c, t approaches zero

The numbers within the matrix are the times (in years) as measured by the traveler, which progressively decrease as the speed of the traveler increases toward the speed of light.

Distance to be traveled in *light years*

	5 *l.y.*	10 *l.y.*	50 *l.y.*	100 *l.y.*	500 *l.y.*	1000 *l.y.*
Speed (fraction of c)						
0.010000000 - i.e. 1%	499.9750	999.9500	4999.7500	9999.5000	49997.4999	99994.9999
0.100000000	49.7494	99.4987	497.4937	994.9874	4974.9372	9949.8744
0.500000000	8.6603	17.3205	86.6025	173.2051	866.0254	1732.0508
0.900000000	2.4216	4.8432	24.2161	48.4322	242.1611	484.3221
0.990000000	**0.7125**	1.4249	7.1246	14.2492	71.2461	142.4923
0.999000000	0.2238	**0.4475**	2.2377	4.4755	22.3775	44.7549
0.999900000	0.0707	0.1414	**0.7072**	1.4143	7.0716	14.1432
0.999990000	0.0224	0.0447	0.2236	**0.4472**	2.2361	4.4722
0.999999000	0.0071	0.0141	0.0707	0.1414	**0.7071**	1.4142
0.999999900	0.0022	0.0045	0.0224	0.0447	0.2236	**0.4472**
0.999999990	0.0007	0.0014	0.0071	0.0141	0.0707	0.1414
0.999999999	0.0002	0.0004	0.0022	0.0045	0.0224	0.0447
At c–1 MPH (in l.y.):						
0.999999998507	0.0003	0.0005	0.0027	0.0055	0.0273	0.0546
At c–1 MPH (in days):						
0.999999998507	0.10	0.20	1.00	1.99	9.97	**19.95**

The numbers within the last row are given in days, and indicate, for example as shown in bold, that at the *speed-of-light* minus *one-mile-per-hour*, the traveler would experience just under 20 days in travel time to cross 1000 light years of distance in space. His actual time as measured in the non-moving frame of reference is still 1000 years, but he only experiences the *dilated* time in his moving frame of reference of about 20 days. In other words, he only ages 20 days. This calculation excludes acceleration (and deceleration) time, which would add additional duration to the trip as experienced by the traveler depending on how rapidly this near-light speed is achieved. Hence, there is no need to postulate a fictional faster-than-light "warp" speed to cross vast distances of space in a normal life span. The amount of time Columbus aged in crossing from Spain to America, at this speed, could be used to travel to the stars in the Orion constellation, and look no worse for wear. The numbers shown in bold along the diagonal in the matrix are travel times under 1 year.

For example, traveling at 99.9999998507 percent of the speed of light, 1000 light years of distance (i.e. from Earth to the stars of the Orion constellation) can be traversed in 20 days. This is the aging the traveler would experience once accelerated to the given speed. There would be additional time from the acceleration and deceleration, which depends on the how quickly one reaches this target speed, and slows down from it. However, this is just a matter of how much energy one is willing to spend, and its related costs and technological capacity to accelerate at high rates. Of course, the time elapsed at the origin and destination would be no less in years than the number of light years of distance. The traveler might only age 20 days, but time will have progressed by 1000 years at the planet of origin and destination. For example, if Jesus Christ or another traveler were to have left Earth 2000 years ago on a craft and accelerated to this speed, then slowed down and stopped a 1000 light years away, then reversed course and accelerated back to the same speed and returned to Earth, then about 2000 years would have elapsed but he would have aged only 40 days – or perhaps a bit more if one adds the time and aging due to the two acceleration and two deceleration events during this roundtrip. The point is that the trip can easily be accomplished within a fraction of a normal lifetime of the traveler; however, don't expect to find your spouse, children or friends alive when you return, unless your trip was to the nearby Zeta Reticuli system, a mere 36 light years away.

Another aspect of this type of travel is that the traveler should not expect to go and return to the same society. The civilization will change between successive visits, and a traveler who leaves Earth for a 72 light year roundtrip should go knowing that he could return no less than 72 years later, even though he or she may age only a fraction of a year. But that is okay. Civilizations progress and thrive over thousands of years, and interaction and travel between them can take place by understanding that once one leaves, if he or she wishes to go far and return, it may be a different age at a different century. If one is to accept this realization, than cosmic travel is no problem, and there are no physical laws preventing it.

Einstein's Theory of Religion is less well known. It was a very unusual belief system that was misunderstood by some and discounted by others, because it did not fit within the established fold of the early-to-mid 20th century. Though he was of Jewish origins, he fits more into a mold that is presently called "Pantheistic" – defined by Wikipedia as follows:

Pantheism is the view that everything is of an all-encompassing immanent abstract God; or that the Universe, or nature, and God are equivalent. More detailed definitions tend to emphasize the idea that natural law, existence, and the Universe (the sum total of all that is, was, and shall be) is represented in the theological principle of an abstract 'god' rather than a personal, creative deity or deities of any kind.

Einstein religious statements are quoted in numerous books by authors such as Richard Dawkins (*The God Delusion*) and Max Jammer (*Einstein and Religion*), some of which are given below:

> *I don't try to imagine a personal God; it suffices to stand in awe at the structure of the world, insofar as it allows our inadequate sense to appreciate it.*
>
> —Albert Einstein

> *Science without religion is lame, religion without science is blind.*
>
> —Albert Einstein

> *It was, of course, a lie what you read about my religious convictions, a lie which is being systematically repeated. I do not believe in a personal God and I have never denied this but have expressed it clearly. If something is in me which can be called religious then it is the unbounded admiration for the structure of the world so far as our science can reveal it.*
>
> —Albert Einstein

I am a deeply religious nonbeliever. This is a somewhat new kind of religion. I have never imputed to Nature a purpose or a goal, or anything that could be understood as anthropomorphic. What I see in Nature is a magnificent structure that we can comprehend only very imperfectly, and that must fill a thinking person with a feeling of humility. This is a genuinely religious feeling that has nothing to do with mysticism. The idea of a personal God is quite alien to me and seems even naive.

—Albert Einstein

Did God have a choice in creating the Universe?

—Albert Einstein

To sense that behind anything that can be experienced there is a something that our mind cannot grasp and whose beauty and sublimity reaches us only indirectly and as a feeble reflection, this is religiousness. In this sense I am religious.

—Albert Einstein

Hence, Einstein thought of Nature, and the laws that govern the universe as the supreme power, which is worthy of our unbounded admiration and humility. Dr. Einstein posed the question of whether God had a choice in creating the universe. By this he meant 'Could the universe have begun in any other way?' Einstein was using 'God' in a purely metaphorical, poetic sense. Like Darwin, Einstein was convinced that laws of nature guide the advancement and unfolding of the physical and biological world, and that assigning a mind to this process is an anthropomorphism – an artificially projected human-like characteristic.

Similarly, Einstein did not believe in a 'personal God' – one who listens to prayers or converses with individuals, and hands out judgments. Praying to God is no more useful than praying to Gravity, but the 'secret' is it motivates one's own self into creative action.

Another of his famous quotes was:

> *I believe in Spinoza's God who reveals himself in the orderly harmony of what exists, not in a God who concerns himself with fates and actions of human beings.*
> —Albert Einstein

This is reflected by another pantheistic thinker: Dr. Masaharu Taniguchi, the founder of the Truth of Life (SNI) movement described in Chapter 2. In discussing the requests people make of God, Dr. Taniguchi teaches that: '*If you wish to call on me, first be reconciled with everything in the universe*' and he explains that through this process of reconciliation one may reach and commune with God. The synopsis in both statements above is that the universe and its laws operate as the ultimate power, synonymous with the "God," and the more one understands and works in harmony with and through these laws, the more one can achieve. In other words, these natural laws and principles upon which the universe operates *is* the omnipresent and omnipotent power, which affects everything, and even a very powerful being must abide by them and operate through them. The old paradoxical question: "God created the universe, but who created God?" – can now be answered. From an Einsteinan sence, the natural laws pre-existed the universe and guided its creation. One plus one equaled two even prior to the Big Bang event. If the universe should collapse – which is the subject of a poem at the end of this book – then the natural laws would still exist even if there is no matter for these laws to govern. And later, should a second Big Bang occur and another universe begun, the old natural laws would resume to operate.

Chapter 8 – Modern Evidence of Earth Visitation and Intervention

There is apparently a wide variety of intelligent beings that come to our planet and interact with people and a wide variety of experiences that unfold. The best evidence is presented by the work of such distinguished scientists, researchesrs and authors as Budd Hopkins, Dr. David Jacobs, Dr. Roger Leir, Barbara Lamb, Dr. Cristianne Quiros, and the late Dr. John Mack. Between them, they have investigated and documented several thousand interactions between otherwise perfectly normal human beings of all walks of life, and beings from elsewhere in the nearby cosmos. It would take more pages than this entire book to summarize their findings. However, their work is public information, and as previously stated in the *Forward* of this book, we ask our readers to seek out further evidence based on references as they may require. I have personally met most of these distinguished authors and researchers over the past years, some more than once, and their work is convincing. I have also personally met some of their subjects and those who have given me direct first-hand accounts of their interaction. In my mind, the question was not whether this interaction is real, but how it fits into a greater worldview and paradigm that describes Truth as we can comprehend.

Some of these off-planet originating intelligent races look like us, and are us in the sense of having common cosmic ancestry, and are no more *alien* than Neil Armstrong and Buzz Aldren and the other astronauts who returned from the surface of another heavenly body. However, some of them do not look like us, but I would argue are still not truly alien in the sense that their evolution, like ours, was governed by a uniform set of laws of nature that permeate the universe. Like the islands of the Galapagos, isolated yet connected to the rest of the world, islands of life on the environment of other planets may have evolved in somewhat different directions. What if the forces prevalent in such other environment would favor more reptilian style life? Would reptilian life forms achieve intelligent levels up an evolutionary tree? Sure they would. Why not? If there is no physical law or natural principle that would prohibit it, there is no reason why it could not become. And what if the forces prevalent in an another planetary environment would favor larger eyes and smaller stature, due to prevalent natural lighting conditions from the nearby star, their local sun, or prevalent gravitational forces that happen to be different that that of earth's? Would smaller beings with larger eyes than ours be favored by natural selection and evolve there? Sure they would. And if they are not used to a bright sun, would their skin be more pale and gray? Sure it would. Therefore, they would need to keep out from our direct sun exposure, since even a few seconds of strong sunlight may cause them health problems. And they would need to keep a darkened film on their eyes, an advanced version of sunglasses, to reduce the natural light from our environment reaching their eyes. There are probably as many solutions to intelligent life as there are distinct environments that are stable enough for a long enough period of time to allow such evolution.

It makes scientific sense that the various beings being described by large numbers of independent witnesses through these researchers would exist. And if they have attained sufficient intelligence and technology beyond our present status, that they would come to visit here, well before our level of civilization is capable of going to visit there.

There is only one catch. Given similar circumstances, similar evolutionary solutions will arise. A given protein molecule will tend to conform into a given three-dimensional shape once it is assembled from a sequence of amino acids in similar environments, even opposite sides of the universe. Physical laws and natural principles are uniform across the cosmos, even if we do not understand them completely. Two plus two equals four in every galaxy. If there is something that pre-existed the unfolding of this universe, it is the physical laws and natural principles upon which it is based. We hold these truths to be self-evident that physical laws and natural principles are equally valid across all parts of the universe, that among these are the principles of cause and affect, mathematics and the laws of biochemistry. And therefore, all intelligent life that evolved under similar (though not identical) environments across the universe would develop to have certain aspects and solutions in common. For instance, living in a gravitational environment surrounded by gaseous oxygen, they would all develop lungs, blood and a heart-like pump, a head on top with most senses terminating near a there-enclosed brain, and two of several things such as legs, arms and eyes, not to mention such basic commonalities as DNA. Whether their evolutionary paths end up with equal number of fingers, details of eye structure or proportion of limbs is not consequential, and likely different. And not surprisingly, the variation in the described visiting beings tend to be just that – basically humanoid with differences in the length, style and number of fingers, type of eyes and pupils, form of head and limbs, type of skin, but basically variations of the same natural solution for a being.

Based on the cumulative results of the above-named researchers, they naturally have other things in common with us as well. One of these is the instinct for self-preservation, for love of life, and behavior based on logic and sometimes emotion. The united theme in the interaction with the various species and races of extraterrestrial origin has been the preservation of the environment of the Earth. Pollution and degradation to the diversity of life in Earth's environments has been a common theme, as has been the promulgation of acceptable social rules of conduct. They want us to behave in ways that prevent destruction to this biosphere. They value it more than us, in the sense that they understand how important and precious a biosphere such as ours is. Unlike the *Prime Directive* envisioned by Gene Roddenberry which prohibits interference of a higher civilization to a lower, less advanced one, their rules apparently require that they intervene is specific ways:

1. Intervene by providing impulses to guide and steer societies.
2. Avoid direct and continuous dictatorial-style governing.
3. Make contacts that are secretive and covert which achieve their purpose without adversely affecting the lives or health of the individuals chosen for such interaction.

4. Continue to work with a select group and their offspring, and qualify new individuals based on genetic and physical criterion.
5. Promote actions which reduce adverse impacts to Earth's environment and "her" ability to support a diverse range of life;
   a. Promote human spiritual growth;
   b. Provide social and moral rules of conduct, sometimes under the guise of seeding religious belief systems with a reward / punishment structure;
   c. Work to reduce the human population on the planet;
   d. For purposes of "insurance" as some researchers call it, for long-term survival of intelligent life on the planet, some of the extraterrestrial races (though not all) are running a process to genetically alter humanity by infusing beneficial genes from their race and create a new hybrid human form;
   e. Interfere where required and where they can with natural volcanic and human nuclear threats to the Earth's biosphere.

Evidence for the above activity is clear and convincing when the information from the listed researchers and others who have investigated the interactions is considered together as a whole. Please review the work for yourself of these wonderful pioneering researchers. Our purposes again, in this book, is not to provide the detailed evidence to convince those who are unwilling or not ready to accept these truths, but to weave together the information from extraterrestrial interactions and religions to provide a new framework view of reality that is self-consistent and unifying, which resolves the differences between the world's major religions and thereby promotes global peace.

CHAPTER 9 – ORIGIN OF RELIGIONS – FROM JEHOVAH TO CHRIST TO MUHAMMAD – A CONTINUUM OF GUIDANCE

Jehovah is also referred to as JHWH, with other pronunciations such as Yahweh to fill in the consonants of these four letters with reasonable vowels. This reference may actually be a title, or rank, rather than a proper name, and refers to the leader who is elected as the most wise of a group of long lived extraterrestrial human beings. This rank or title means 'king of wisdom' and is passed from generation to generation amongst this group. According to the writings of a well-known Swiss farmer who describes many years of contacts with this group of human beings known as Plajeren or Pleiadian, there is a present day leader who bears the rank of JHWH whose proper name is Ptaah, and is over 770 (earth) years old. According to Ptaah, as quoted in the book *And Still They Fly*, this rank was abused in the past as would a "despotic ruler whose power corrupted his judgment." The leader who we know as Jehovah or Yahweh of course had good intentions, which is to select and guide a society of early Earth's population whom he felt was worthy, and shield them against outside injustice purported upon them by other peoples and societies or nations. However, as we so well know from the Old Testament, He became impatient with the lack of continued devotion or adherence to his guidance by the later generations and attempted to scatter his originally beloved people as punishment.

Power corrupts, even with the best of intentions and cosmic plans. But when the plans involve the cultural engineering and moral guidance of the early societies of a planet, the wrongs must be righted. Even those with the rank of JHWH must evolve and better themselves. As we said in the last chapter, it may not be quite like the *prime directive* where interference of a higher civilization with a lower one is forbidden, but more like a timely correction of one leader who succeeds an earlier one and attempts to correct his transgression of inappropriate or overzealous guidance. Make no mistake, the task of that JHWH we know as Jehovah was a colossal undertaking, no less in scope than to build the foundations of a civilization which was to live by the laws of nature, thereby setting it on a straight and narrow path of long term advancement and survival.

For additional information on JHWH, we look at translated scrolls know as the Talmud of Jmmanuel (or Emanuel – a name by which Jesus was also known), and the Muslim Holy Qur'an (or Koran). These texts have valuable descriptions that bring the puzzle of cosmic guidance to more modern times.

There were three sets of lost religious scrolls found in the 20th century:
1. The Nag-Hammadi Library, found in Egypt in 1945
2. The Dead Sea Scrolls, found in Israel in 1947
3. The Talmud of Jmmanuel, found in Israel in 1963

According to the Talmud of Jmmanuel, which parallels

the traditional Gospel of Matthew and the other books of the New Testament that chronicle the life of Jesus, the true biological father of Jesus was Gabriel. In Chapter 1 verse 82-88, this supposedly unchanged text from around the 1st century AD tell how Joseph was filled with wrath and thought of leaving Mary when he heard of her secret impregnation by a descendant of the celestial sons who came far from the depths of space. But when he was thinking in this way, he was visited by a "guardian angel, sent by Gabriel, the celestial son who had impregnated Mary" and said to him that *"Mary is betrothed to you, and you are to become her spouse; do not leave her, because the fruit of her womb is chosen for a great purpose."* These verses also give a year of eleven thousand years from the time when Adam was procreated between an Earth woman of an indigenous race and another celestial son who came from afar in the cosmos. Later in Chapter 3 verses 30-34, it states that after Jesus was baptized by John in the Jordan river, a metallic light flew over them and the voice of Gabriel said *"this is my beloved son with whom I am well pleased. He will be the king of truth, through which terrestrial humans shall rise as wise ones."* Correlating to the official Biblical canon, after Jesus was baptized in the Jordan by John, "coming up out of the water, he saw the heavens opened, and the Spirit like a dove descending upon him; and there came a voice from heaven, saying, *Thou art my beloved Son, in whom I am well pleased."* (Mark 1:10-11) In comparing these two passages, it is clear that the official canon may be interpreted as God speaking to his son Jesus, whereas in the Talmud of Jmmanuel, Chapter 3, this interaction is clarified as between Jesus and his actual biological father Gabriel.

Later in Chapter 30, verses 47 and 48, it is described that Jesus cried out on the cross then his head fell forward, he slipped into a state of near-death, and they presumed he was dead. In Chapter 30, verse 65, it is stated that Joseph and friends of Jesus from India entered his tomb through a secret second passage and nursed Him back to health over the course of three days. Chapter 33 describes how Jesus went to Damascus, Syria, after leaving Judea and spent two years there. Chapter 35 describes how He then traveled with his mother to the "cities at the sea in the north" and continued to teach. In chapter 36, the last translated chapter of the Talmud of Jmmanuel, it is described that Jesus then traveled by caravan toward the East. In the Epilogue of the scrolls which describe the content of other chapters that were not translated, it states that Jesus traveled to the Kashmir region of India where he had a family and continued to teach under a different identity until his natural death at about age 110 – 115.

Switching to the Holy Qur'an, Chapter 4 verse 157, there is a corroborating section that states: *'And their saying: Surely we have killed the Messiah, Isa son of Marium, the apostle of Allah; and they did not kill him nor did they crucify him, but it appeared to them so, and most surely those who differ therein are only in a doubt about it; they have no knowledge respecting it, but only follow a conjecture, and they killed him not for sure."* The Qur'an Chapter 97 verse 4, also names Gabriel as the teacher of Muhammad. Speaking of the grand night of revelation, this verse states *"The angels and Gibreel descend in it by the permission of their Lord for every affair".* Therefore, the long-lived celestial son Gabriel was not only the biological father of Him we know as Jesus

Christ, but several hundred years later (at about 610 AD) was also responsible for giving the teachings to the Arabic people through their prophet Muhammad.

In this way, Gabriel corrected the misdeeds of his predecessor JHWH known as Lord God, Yahweh or Jehovah, by bringing the moral guidance and teachings to yet other people in other cultures. He fathered his own son through Mary and taught him, which became Christianity. He then chose Muhammad and revealed the teachings to him as well, somewhat modified and arranged to be appropriate to that culture at that time. Hence the teachings of the Old Testament, New Testament, and the Holy Qur'an are related, and represent moral rules and behavioral guidance passed down from the Plejaren people, human beings with whom we share common cosmic ancestry. He also corrected misconceptions which ended up in the New Testament and hence Christianity, with respect to the apparent death of his son on the crucifix, a statement that corroborates the events as described in the Talmud of Jmmanuel scrolls, which specifically describe Gabriel as a descendent of the people who came from the Seven Stars, or the Pleiades, and who are also known as the Plejaren.

Here is a figure representing the approximate lifespan of the various kings of wisdom in the course of extraterrestrial interventions, two of whom spawned the three major religions of Judaism, Christianity and Islam:

Figure 1: Approximate timescale of JHWH extraterrestrial leaders

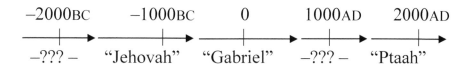

Buddhism had a major resurgence and restatement in the 1st century AD, in Kashmir, India. According to the Talmud of Jmmanuel, Chapter 20, Verse 28 and also the Gnostic Bible, Jesus taught reincarnation. This was of course withdrawn from the Christian canon in subsequent centuries, most likely in the fourth century by Constantine; however, it is preserved in these older set of scrolls. According to the Talmud of Jmmanuel, Jesus did not teach that he was the son of God, as given in the modern Christian canon, but that he was a man, descendant of Gabriel and Mary. He also taught that Creation is to be revered, and the natural laws and principles upon which Creation is based. From this perspective, his teaching becomes more similar to Buddhism than to modern Christianity, whereby there is no supreme God who created the Creation where we live once and go to heaven or hell, but rather, where we are part of the grand Creation where we pass through multiple life times of learning, achieving a higher level of spirituality through each reincarnation. His teachings, and therefore the Plejaren teachings, would have then played a major role in the religion we refer to in modern days as Buddhism. This would then tie the four major religions to a common origin. Buddhism and Hinduism both have roots in India. I leave it to the reader to make this final connection to the fifth major religion of today's world.

The root teachings encompassed by the Ten Commandmants, especially the later seven, the teachings of Jesus, especially in his reverence to the Creation without the concept of God the creator as revealed in the Talmud of Jmmanuel, the teachings of the Holy Qur'an which detail these moral teachings in the context of the Arab culture, and those of Buddhism with its principles of physical moderation and spiritual reincarnation would then give us a glimpse of the moral and spiritual belief system of our extraterrestrial friends. We could rightfully refer to this as *Cosmic Religion*, although they would object by pointing out that the word *Religion* is in itself misleading. What makes sense, however, is that certain basic rules of conduct for intelligent life would be universal – as universal as the basic principles of biochemistry that governs the behavior of protein molecules uniformly from one side of the universe to the other. Basic rules of morality that teach such things as not to extinguish or misuse life and its processes must apply to all intelligent life across the cosmos. Whether one misapplies the energies locked in the atom to extinguish a biosphere on this planet or another planet a million light years away would be just as negative of an affect on the spark of life throughout the vast cosmic creation, and the progress of life would be just as bright.

The more similar a life form is to another, the more they feel akin and apt to help each other. We should thank our extraterrestrial cousins for assisting our moral and spiritual development over the different centuries and different cultures, as bizarre as this may sound, and stop our insignificant arguments over our apparent religious differences through realizing that these belief systems basically have common origins, from which they naturally diverged over time and across cultures. There is only one catch: to enable us to return to our roots and reunite these dispersed belief systems, we must first come to understand our extraterrestrial cosmic ancestry. The longer we take to bite the bullet to do this, the longer world peace will take. Ironically, our science fiction writers once postulated that a common cosmic enemy might unite all mankind in a common defense. But this is a delusion. Fear of our extraterrestrial cousins is a misplaced emotion, no matter how scary they may appear, or how well this fear sells Hollywood movies. It is like fearing our own father or mother when they discipline us, rather than realize that their actions are based in love and care. Until we collectively come to terms with this expanded worldview from a proper perspective, world peace may have to wait. Once we accept these visitors for who they are, world peace will come naturally without trying.

CHAPTER 10 – PROTECTING THE EARTH FROM MAN

According to the U.S. constitution, "We hold these truths to be *self-evident*, that all men are created equal, that they are endowed by their Creator with certain unalienable Rights, that among these are Life, Liberty and the pursuit of Happiness." This statement can be taken a few steps further. Even aliens have unalienable rights. Since they appear to be just a different race, they would also be endowed by the Creator, with perhaps the same Life, Liberty and the pursuit of Happiness that we claim for ourselves. But what if these attributes require for them to intervene in our earthly affairs? What if our destructive ways on this planet adversely affects their life and pursuit of happiness? The Earth may not be the only inhabited planet in the universe, or even in this region of our galaxy, but it is still unique and very precious. Should our present civilization destroy the biosphere, or even the entire planet, it would surely be a great loss for the collection of life in this region of the cosmos. It's loss may have a devastating ripple effect for sentient life elsewhere, and this life from afar may therefore have a stake and vested interest in preventing it. Biodiversity and the health of the various ecosystems in our biosphere are of paramount importance and fundamental value to this region of the galaxy, if not the whole universe.

Past and vastly wiser civilizations from elsewhere in the cosmos would know how civilizations generally grow and mature. They would have seen it, and recorded it as cosmic history on a grand time scale. They would have known that civilizations reach a certain technological age where the understanding of the natural laws and their immature application can wield vast destruction. Therefore, they would want to guide a budding civilization toward proper growth, and guide it early on, well before it acquires sufficient knowledge of natural laws to wield vast technological power. For history repeats itself, even on a grand cosmic scale. Given equivalent circumstances, the law of cause and effect would yield equivalent outcomes. Not only would they learn from the possible downfall of prior cosmic civilizations, but they would know the approximate time line, and the general sequence of events. Based on this prior knowledge, it is reasonable that they would know it takes just about the equivalent time of two millennia to evolve technological progress from the time and circumstances of the civilization around our Mediterranean Sea at the time of Christ, or about fifteen hundred years from the time of Muhammad. So they could appear to predict what happens in our future, from back then. They could write down predictions as given in the later sections of the Bible, projected to be approximately in our present time. They could however not know or predict the exact passage of time to specific future events, but they could point to "signs" that precede such events. And they could communicate with selected members of our civilization we call prophets to have these predictions written down for us centuries if not epochs in advance.

It is said that we now live in the end times. What does this really mean? Their predictions and forecasts based on their prior knowledge of the kinetics of civilizations has projected that upon control of nuclear power and space flight, a civilization unchecked will self-destruct through war and environmental repercussions. Most people would sadly agree. A punishing God is not required to carry out such a sentence. The natural laws that govern the universe both physically and sociologically will carry out the sentence. But the key word is "unchecked" – for a major intervention that checks the otherwise destructive sequence of events can change the outcome. It may be the end of an epoch and life and civilization as we know it, though what is coming is simply not written down for us to know in our holy books. If it were, it would interfere with the guidance and the necessary affects of the bitter pill which our civilization must next swallow.

Chapter 11 – Hybrid Children and the Future of Homo Sapiens

One of the authors referenced in Chapter 8 before was Cristianne Quiros. She was granted her PhD based on her thesis entitled "Exo-Psychology Research: A Phenomenological Study of People Who Believe Themselves to be Alien-Human Hybrids." In summary, her research focused on six female adults who believe themselves to be alien-human hybrids, and have various physiological differences to support their beliefs. Cristianne had interviewed these participants and synthesized an understanding about them in her PhD dissertation. Here is what she concluded in the final paragraphs of her thesis …

> "Perhaps we are in training for full-on ET contact. Maybe unconsciously we are seeking them. And what we find as contact increases is both more remarkable and more intrinsic to humankind than we have ever begun to imagine.
>
> "If we are indeed interfertile with the aliens, we are still children of the same Grand Creator. Can we look into the eyes of hybrids and begin to discover the deep wonders of cosmobiology? Or will our fears and limitations make us want to confine or destroy them? Our world is changing rapidly. Those who can bend, flex, and flow with these changes are more likely to survive. Those who are rigid and cannot incorporate the changes will be caught by their own terror and inability to adapt.
>
> – Cristianne Quiros

Christianne details accounts of babies who were born appearing slightly different than normal babies, and behaving as if more intelligent than newborn or young children should be. She describes events of apparent impregnation that occurred almost immaculately, and were masked with memories of normal sex or choreographed as if to occur within normal relationships that happened more extraordinarily, under extraterrestrial control and procedures. These conceptions are not unlike the immaculate conception of Jesus described in the Bible, and her dissertation describes some subtle differences that tend to distinguish hybrid children. One such child started talking at three months of age, and could carry on an intelligent conversation in full sentences before becoming one year old. That particular child is now an adult, and has received her own PhD in international studies. She believes that her purpose in life is to become an international ambassador for helping global pollution. Most hybrids seem to have such a specific purpose or mission, and it is often related to the environment. They are often good communicators and have more psychic, empathic and telepathic abilities than most of us.

Similar evidence from other researchers of both M.D. and Ph.D. stature seem to be consistent in describing a widespread extraterrestrial program of creating hybrid human children, where a portion of the genetic makeup is directly of extraterrestrial ancestry. Dr. David Jacobs in his published work describes so called "late generation hybrids" that are more viable as living beings than early generation hybrids such as those of a 50% – 50% parentage. He gives many eyewitness testimonies that describe direct

50% hybrids as frail, and with very alien-like appearance. However, after about four or five generations with human parentage, the late generation hybrid children appear virtually indistinguishable from a standard human being, except for some tell-tale signs that only a trained person can distinguish. The early stage hybrids need to grow up and live in an extraterrestrial artificial environment specific to our alien guests; however, the later stage hybrids can live amongst us in our environment. Some of them know that they are part of a grand program of genetic change, and are in continuous contact with their alien culture; whereas, others as described by Dr. Quiros live amongst us and only suspect their special heritage. Based on the scrolls described in Chapter 9 called the Talmud of Jmmanuel, Jesus himself knew of his hybrid parentage, with his father Gabriel being one of the descendants of the Plajerans. This information was deleted from the official canon. Jesus is quoted in these scrolls as saying that we will only know the truth about his parentage and real self in the days following the advent of space travel by human technology, not to mention the advent of genetic engineering.

There are descriptions of hybrid human children with various different extraterrestrial races by different researchers. After multiple generations with increasing percentage of human ancestry, they all converge on a rather human appearance, but maintain aspects of their alien genetics and abilities. One such characteristic as described by most researchers is in the arena of mental abilities, as in being more psychic and telepathic. In fact, the vast majority of members of our normal human race who report contact and are affected by the alien abduction phenomenon report that they have an increase in their telepathic abilities through training by these human or not-so-human beings. The extraterrestrial races who appear least human are reported to communicate almost exclusively through telepathic contact, and through these interactions, the human subjects affected are forced to develop these innate but unused skills. At first, such communication is described as "voices speaking in my head" in the language of the human subjects. When they respond with spoken words, they are invariably instructed to "think" or subvocalize their responses, which is then understood. After some training, some subjects report "feeling" the approaching presence of a familiar extraterrestrial being by a telepathic sense that precedes direct telepathic communication or conversation. In some reports, an advanced being with strong mental capabilities can be so overwhelming to a nearby human being that he or she has difficulty in concentrating on their own thoughts and state of consciousness without the interference of the overbearing mental presence. The parallels to the descriptions of Moses and other prophets hearing the voice of God speak from within is quite remarkable.

Enhanced telepathic abilities is an obvious advantage from an evolutionary perspective if a civilization is to survive wars and conflict. Taken to the extreme, this ability would eliminate all secrecy. Adversaries would instantly "hear" their opponent's plan and strategy, and be able to immediately apply countermeasures. In essence, the ability to wage war or even maintain conflicts would diminish with the level of telepathic ability. Of course, we are speaking now of a mass genetic shift in the human population, which provides for the enhanced structure within the nervous system to enable or increase our innate abilities and skills in this regard. The present form of homo sapiens of all major races on earth are lacking in these capabilities, some races lacking more than others. Given enough time, the genetic enhancements may spread across our population and lead to a new mankind that protects the Earth, and lives in harmony within the greater environment.

There is only one problem in this genetic intervention program. The process may be too slow in relation to the increase in potentially devastating technology and planetary environmental degradation. In scientific terms, the frequency of such telepathic endowing alleles in the genome of the greater population may advance slower than required for the intended effect of changing overall behavior. The greater the size of the population, the slower the genetic overhaul. So overpopulation is a hindrance to this process. Fortunately for our extraterrestrial guides the problem may be self-correcting in that backlash of the environmental degradation would naturally be a reduction in birthrate and reduction in life sustenance for the population. Should the size of our population on Earth significantly drop due to changes in the environment, in climate, and possibly nuclear wars, a resurgence of a new and genetically modified population can be effected. Those on Earth who have already been shifted genetically or are sufficiently advanced in their cultural understanding and intelligence to fit within the new civilization can be extracted from the worsening environmental conditions. And the world would end as we know it, as metaphorically written in the Bible and other prophetic religious texts.

I have personally been to both Hiroshima and Nagasaki. It was most interesting to see that after fifty years there is virtually no sign that a major nuclear devastation had taken place. So it is possible to recover relatively quickly in historic time from major destruction, whether due to natural environmental causes or intelligently controlled technology at its worst. After those nuclear events, it was believed that not a blade of grass would grow at the center of those unfortunate cities for seventy-five years, and the area would remain dangerously radioactive and remain unable to support life for a very long time. This did not happen, and both cities are back to their splendor as if the nuclear destruction had never occurred. Modern day Pompeii has also recovered. The effect that these volcanic and nuclear destructions did have is that they instantly eliminated a vast amount of life and population. They wiped out existing population of the regions, yet allowed new populations to move in fairly quickly from a historical time perspective. Widespread Earth changes and nuclear wars may have the same effect, on a global scale. And thereafter, in a relatively brief time on a geologic scale, the environment can mend, and a new population that is more empathetic to the biosphere with less tendency to wage war can be replanted. This new population may even represent a sufficient shift in the genotype and phenotype of the inhabitants to possibly warrant a new name beyond that of Homo Sapiens.

CHAPTER 12 – THE FUTURE –
A COSMIC HUMANITY

In 1971, a visionary song writer wrote these lyrics:

Imagine there's no heaven
It's easy if you try
No hell below us
Above us only sky
Imagine all the people
Living for today...
Imagine there's no country
It isn't hard to do
Nothing to kill or die for
And no religion too
Imagine all the people
Living life in peace...

– *Imagine*, by John Lenon

In my mind this sentiment echoes the aspiration for peace and harmony with the whole universe. If you, the reader, understands the premise laid out in this book about why and how religions were likely introduced to Earth, then you will see beyond the need for blind faith, you will see the irony in immature statements like "God give me this... God please grant that..." and you will realize a higher plane of spirituality and perspective. Leapfrogging beyond the Copernican revolution that our Sol is the center of the universe, we can come to accept that our life on Earth is not unique in the universe. We can come to understand a unified worldview that brings together our observations of the cosmos and the roots of culture, and creates a self-consistent comprehension of terrestrial and extraterrestrial intelligent life. We can understand the hopes and actions of those who guided us under the pretense of being an almighty deity and see past the allegories and half-truths of the religious texts to cast out our delusions. We can discard the obscure idea that countries and religions should run our lives and understand the immutable laws of nature across our cosmic environment and strive to act in harmony with them. We should not need a fearful concept of hell or an enticing heaven if we can just live in harmony with nature and all life in the biosphere. We must realize that we are all one in a grand wave of existence, and our apparently individual minds form a sea of consciousness.

We should put aside 'God' and just focus on being thankful and in harmony with All there is. We should be citizens of the world, and then citizens of the cosmos, and act for the betterment of all life in the universe. If we can be comfortable in this grand worldview, then everything from the mysteries of the holy texts to the secret enigma of intelligently controlled flying objects from elsewhere will make sense in a concerted mental model of reality. We have to forgive Jehovah for the cruelty he inspired, and for the deception he played on the human culture he tried to guide, because his successors did their best to mitigate his errors. And finally we have to accept the response of nature and the intertwined series of causes and effects that reflects each of our actions back onto us as if an almighty intelligence was at work. And we have to put ourselves in the shoes of our not-so-alien guides and see their point of view in trying yet another intervention to modify humanity with new traits that will improve Earth's survival. Their survival may be linked to our survival, and so their actions are justified.

Religion has served its purpose in the past by instilling fear of a grand power within the universe if people deviate from the commandments handed down. It has now outlived its usefulness, and we must recognize that the real reason to keep laws and commandments is to be harmonious with nature and the whole universe. There is no hell, heaven, divine stick or divine carrot, only universal love and joy that results from complete harmony and peace with all people, all things, and the whole universe itself. Though some may continue to use the word 'God' since most people on Earth cannot yet grasp a Creation without a 'Creator', our mental model of reality will be more true and correct without this reference. Instead of saying: "God is All of everything; God is absolute and dwells in all things," try thinking that: "Creation is All of everything; and the natural laws dwell and operate in all things." The method by which Creation unfolded itself is not necessarily by divine design but simply by adhering to the pre-existing set of natural laws, whether the human mind can comprehend them in entirety. We can certainly comprehend much of these, and classify them under titles such as mathematics, physics, chemistry and biochemistry. The more highly complex biological systems of course have intelligence and self-awareness, and there are natural laws that govern the interaction of individual self-aware beings, whether human or more distant on the evolutionary tree. The natural laws dictate the optimal form of such intelligent beings, with a head on top and two arms and two legs. The variation in number of fingers or the range of wavelengths their eyes respond to are dependent on local evolutionary factors. But the basic solution for the form of an intelligent being living in a field of gravity would be uniform. In a sense, the term 'alien' is relative, and we are all brothers and cousins in the grand cosmic evolution of life, during the present cycle of this Universe, since the most recent Big Bang.

As my personal journey neared completion in the Galapagos Islands on my trustworthy trimaran sailboat during February of 2005, my mind felt clear and awestruck with the vast variation of life forms. I visited Darwin Island and Wolf Island and swam alone amongst beautiful hammerhead sharks, which hardly noticed me. I kayaked the rouged coastlines and observed the aquatic iguanas and unusual birds. I met the oldest known living animal on Earth – a Galapagos tortoise – who seemed to nod his head towards me. I felt this cradle of life and instinctively knew without a doubt that such life abound elsewhere beyond Earth where similar conditions existed. I could even sense that at this very moment, on another similar planet, dinosaurs are now alive and thriving. After all they had a very successful run that lasted far longer than the span of human existence on this planet. The probability of dinosaurs living on a distant planet would therefore be greater than that of intelligent life. And we can now surmise that intelligent life must also live elsewhere, since our cosmic visitors must come from somewhere. Furthermore, if the variety of alien races witnessed by many are as diverse out there as amongst those visiting and interacting with some of us, then the diversity of intelligent life in the cosmos must be even greater, as long as they all have a head and two arms and two legs, or a head and assorted fins.

Chapter 13 – What Does This All Mean to Our Daily Lives?

A religion or philosophy without daily guidance in our lives is merely an academic interest. Isa said: "*The truth will set you free.*" But what exactly does this mean? When the truth potentially turns our worldview upside down, how will it set us free? A new paradigm is perhaps more stress than the relaxing bliss that the word *freedom* implies. It is stressful to our scientific perspectives and stressful to our sense of origins. It stresses our very belief of why we are here. What then does the truth about our origins and our link to intelligent life in the cosmos enable us to do?

The world famous physicist Stephen Hawking said at a March 2009 public lecture in Pasadena, California: "*Watch out if you meet an alien – you could be infected with a pathogen against which you have no resistance.*"
Dr. Hawking also said that *intelligence* may not be an evolutionary selective force. Bacterial and other lower life forms are far more likely to be found on other planets in the cosmos than intelligent life, because intelligent life tends to destroy itself. It has the ability to destroy its environment much more so than bacteria, plants or lower animal life, since these are forced to live in harmony and balance within their environment. This is indeed a scary thought. Just look how much longer dinosaurs existed on Earth in comparison to us. It took a rare natural disaster to wipe them out, but in a few short centuries we have come to understand and control the forces of nature to amass nuclear weapons that if activated has far more destructive

effect than that meteorite. If we were to detonate just a few nuclear devices at the base of major volcanoes on the planet, the resulting eruptions, tidal effects and tectonic plate disruptions would precipitate a calamity far worse than did that meteor to the dinosaurs. Earth's orbit may become an asteroid field, similar to the one at 2.7 AU outside the orbit of Mars, where a planet should be.

The world famous biologist Francis Crick, co-discoverer of DNA, calculated the odds that even the simplest sequence of polynucleotides required to code for the simplest of organisms could have occurred on Earth by evolutionary chance. His answer seemed to indicate such a low probability that he felt that life must have been planted here, in the form of DNA sequences appropriate to the early Earth environment. This is the theory of *panspermia*. Life then further evolved in this new environment, except for certain jumps like primates to human, a transition for which there is very scarce fossil record as would be required by evolution. Taken together, these indicate that there were several interventions from the cosmos to direct life on this planet. Again, what does this mean to our daily lives and as to how we should conduct ourselves?

The answer to all these questions is, ironically, found in the common religious teachings. Why? Not simply because they are the word of "God" – but because those teachings have been given to us by our fellow intelligent brothers and cousins from the cosmos, giving us direction in the only "name" by which we might understand their origin. They were addressing us at the level of our intellect. If they say to Moses, follow the fire by night and the cloud by day, because the almighty commands you, they will follow. If they say to him that they are advanced human brothers from elsewhere in the cosmos with advanced technical capabilities, the Hebrews would be less likely to follow, and more likely to question many things.

The intelligent beings that have guided us in the name of God were generally beneficent, especially to those they focused and concentrated their efforts toward. The prophets through whom they spoke, in a way anonymously, have recorded teachings that are valid. These teachings are based on universal principles of life which our cosmic benefactors have learned from their much longer histories than we have at our disposal. Concepts such as *love thy neighbor as thyself* and *be ye merciful, as your Father also is merciful* and *ye do unto him, as he had thought to have done unto his brother* and *do unto him even as he shall say unto thee* – are all universal teachings. The later seven of the Ten Commandments are universal, whether taken from "God" or understood as common natural principles by which intelligent living beings should conduct themselves. Islam has just as many such teachings, cast by the same teachers. Among common commandments are to fast, give alms, pray or meditate or have a day of rest, and be fair and just.

If indeed the same teachers handed down our *religious* guiding principles, whether through the prophet Muhammad, Abraham, Isaiah, Moses, Jesus or the Buddha, they are from the same source, and the recipients need not be in competition with each other. Indeed, the most important new principle which we must realize is that the different religious groups need not fight each other. These teachers handed down the universal principles to each group in the language and context in which the various groups would understand the principles. Whether it was through Moses to the Hebrews, through Jesus to what became Christians, or whether it was through Muhammad to the Muslims, or any divergent group within each of these, the intent was to propagate the same universal teachings to all human beings on Earth. This is a very simple truth. How absurd it is that each group should conflict and fight with each other, claiming that their source is the true and only source!

Guidance is naturally communication at a level of understanding that is appropriate to each recipient, and in the language of each recipient. And what's more, the teachings have been perverted to some degree since handed down by the original masters, the original prophets. They have been changed due to human influences, and through the filter of human rulers and governments over the centuries and millennia. So there would appear to be more differences, and more to fight about as to which is the *correct way*.

So I cannot stress highly enough that the realization that all major religions were originally communicated to the various earthly groups at the various times by the same ancient extraterrestrial teachers means that neither religion is better than the other, and it is counterproductive to have the groups fight amongst themselves.

We are all *one*, not necessarily in a strict religious sense, but in the sense that we are all governed by the same universal principles. Not only are we *one* as humanity with a common biological root ancestry on Earth, and not only are we *one* as brothers governed by the same universal principles, but we are also *one* with our extraterrestrial teachers. Our biological roots are their biological roots which we share in common, and the universal principles which they have handed down to us as guidance are also binding upon them. In simple language, not only should we not fight amongst ourselves, we should not fight them. They do not fight amongst themselves, and there are various different extraterrestrial cultures and races. Their empathic and telepathic abilities are greater than ours, and any conflict between their various groups is effectively defused not only by their mutual knowledge of the same universal principles, but also constrained by their lack of secrecy from each other enacted by their mutual telepathic link. Some members of the race we commonly call as Grays have been observed to blink together in simultaneous synchrony. In some encounters with this species, human participants who were able to retain their conscious memory of the event have reported such strong mental activity in the vicinity of a Gray being that they had difficulty focusing on their own will and thoughts. These mental capabilities amongst our extraterrestrial cousins provide an interlink which makes it difficult for them to disagree even if they tried. That level of evolutionary ability appears to provide a safety factor which helps to prevent them from using technological power inappropriately, and drive them to act in consensus with each other, more like a beehive than competing individuals. They act more like *one*, in concert, and wish for us to have more of those advanced genes to make us more telepathic so we can act *one* with them as well. This is a major aim of the hybridization program.

So how do we conduct our daily lives, given the reality of this interaction? In addition to understanding that we, as different religious groups, need not fight amongst ourselves, the second major action we should all undertake is to prove that through this realization we are sufficiently mature to become harmonious with our environment, and not threaten the biosphere of the planet. If we are conjointly successful in this second task, we may relieve their need for the hybridization program, as we may remove the causes that led our environment itself to fight back.

The Earth is not really alive, in the conventional sense of being an organism that is capable of reproduction or that is self-aware. But our Earth is indeed capable of reacting to harmful actions by our species, as well evidenced by the global warming and climate change which we have come to comprehend in the last few years. By us acting in harmony with our planetary environment, our environment will not go out of equilibrium and cause us grief. By understanding that our friendly extraterrestrial guides have been intervening and manipulating the growth of our cultures in the best way they knew how, our friends will no longer have to hide and act secretive. And by stopping what were religious conflicts and wars and behaving more like them as a unified *one*, we may have a chance to convince them that the hybridization program is no longer required, and perhaps avoid or lessen the tribulation and calamity that was forecast in the last book of the Bible.

But perhaps we cannot. In that case, we can at least understand the real reasons for the events that are to follow. Knowing the truth will set us free. If we can act in a way that Seicho-No-Ie describes as in accordance with our God-nature within, in other words act in a way that is consistent with an understanding of the universal principles that guides all of us in the cosmos, then we shall be alright. We should practice the benevolent teachings and commandments of our religious doctrines of love, wisdom and harmony, knowing that the first three of the Ten Commandments and similarly the first Pillar of Islam were simplifications by our extraterrestrial guides using language that we might understand. The remainder of the commandments are valid from the perspective of advocating universal cultural principles which all living societies must live by.

By keeping in mind the greater cosmic perspective, we shall understand the actions and interventions taken by our guides within the various cultures on Earth over all of recorded history. Interventions and miracles can be understood for what they were, and why they were enacted. What appeared to be the chariots of gods in the native cultures across the Americas will also make sense, and tie in with the extraterrestrial interactions in the main world religions. The truth shall set us free, and enlighten us. How many of us longed to be free of oppressive secrecy, will now understand the need that there was for it. The very realization of this new worldview, this paradigm, will in effect lift the biggest secret of the centuries, indeed the secret of many millennia. Male circumcision was not a covenant commanded by an almighty omniscient creator. He would have created men circumcised. It is perhaps the greatest evidence effecting about ten percent of the human inhabitants on Earth that advanced extraterrestrial life, with whom we share common cosmic ancestors, have been guiding and periodically intervening in the growth of our societies and cultures. Their relatively more advanced knowledge of life sciences and technology, together with their cosmic historical perspective on advancing cultures was used to guide us. With over six billion and soon to be seven billion people on this planet, we greatly outnumber them, and do well to heed their guidance. We need to look past the veil of covert interventions and secrecy, and come to terms with the reality that the universe is teeming with life. We should be enlightened enough to know that all living creatures across this vast universe must live in harmony within their own environments, whether primitive or intelligent. Our environment has grown, from villages to city-states to nations to the globe, and if we can embrace and thank our off-world guides without illusions to their true identity, we will no doubt go cosmic.

Chapter 14 – Truth and Post-Traumatic Stress Disorder

One more subject needs to be discussed, and that is the effect of knowing truth. Let's turn to nature for a perspective. Young baby seals have no sense of a true mental image that represents reality. They just respond to stimuli and instinct. They are not afraid of people, and from curiosity and mistaken thinking, they have been known to climb up on kayaks to check out the occupants. It has happened to me on a remote island. The kayak feels like a warm sanctuary, like a smooth rock, and they sniff at you thinking you are their mother, especially when wearing a black wetsuit. There is no stress or trauma on their part, just what we might call ignorant bliss. But try doing this with an older seal! As they learn and form a mental image of reality, they become increasingly afraid of people. Children or young adults are still curious enough to swim close to you, even swim with you, but at a safe distance. As they get older and wiser, they bark at you, and avoid you like a plague. They see you more correctly as a potentially dangerous predator or enemy, and get traumatized if you try to approach.

So it is with some encounters between people, and certainly with encounters between people and our visiting extraterrestrial biologic entities. The greater the difference the more is the fear. The greater the apparent power and abilities of the person or entity that approaches us, the greater the fear, and an encounter is potentially traumatic. When our worldview is suddenly and forcibly shattered, it is traumatic. In the case of interaction between human beings of different moral views of the world, like when the allied forces liberated central Europe at the end of World War II and came upon the death camps, the witnesses were shocked and many were deeply traumatized for life at the reality they saw with their own eyes. Veteran soldiers in general have difficulty in re-integrating within a peaceful society because of what they see and what they are made to do as soldiers. What to them seems "cruel and unusual" treatment was cruel and usual for another culture. Their experiences are sometimes so traumatic that they need psychological treatment to integrate and deal with the new mental images and observations.

In case of encounters with extraterrestrial aliens, the suppressed trauma of those who experienced the abduction encounters and the investigation of their latently surfacing trauma is what actually uncovered the phenomenon. If we could make an adult seal forget that we approached them, their memory would not resurface to traumatize them in the future. If we could make the allied soldiers forget that they ever saw the death camps, the memory of the experience would not resurface to traumatize them throughout the rest of their lives. So it is with our wise and knowledgeable visitors. They calm their human abductees as well as they can during the encounter, and they neurologically suppress the memory of the events in the brains of the abductees as well as they can to prevent future recall of these disturbing truths, so the people can go on with their normal daily lives. Strong trauma from the shock of an expanded reality can paralyze and potentially stop a culture, and they do not want that.

Truth can therefore be devastating. Whether for the seal whose world is threatened by an outsider, or a solder whose world view is shattered by witnessing atrocities, or an otherwise normal human being who is unexpectedly taken into an alien environment and is made to endure an abduction experience. Fortunately, like an anesthesiologist who prevents us from remembering an otherwise painful and traumatic surgery, our extraterrestrial visitors know how to prevent us from remembering an otherwise shocking conscious encounter. And they go through great extents to calm a person at the time of their conscious encounter, when the real-time events are forcefully shattering our view of reality. Thanks for that. We ought to express some gratitude here. Unfortunately, evidenced by the thousands of affected individuals who had sought out therapy, and without knowing each other, independently described very similar events to independent researchers (Benjamin Simon, Budd Hopkins, John Mack, David Jacobs and Barbara Lamb to name a few), the mental blocks imposed by our visitors are somewhat spotty. The thousands whose memories of the events have been uncovered, according to the researchers, may be just the tip of the iceberg with potentially significant percentages of the entire human population affected, whose abduction memories are still suppressed.

In time, new truths can be accepted. As happened with the discoveries of Copernicus and Galileo, at first an idea is resisted, then the idea is actively opposed, and finally the idea is accepted as self-evident. New truths can gradually be incorporated into one's worldview. The masterminds who orchestrated some of the extraordinary and apparently supernatural events recorded in the Old and New Testaments had, I think, intended the true realities behind those events to come through to our understanding in time. They left many clues and parables, but until our recent technological age, those clues could not be interpreted. They wanted us to know the truth when we're ready. We are now ready – or almost ready. Until we are, we have to take the guidance and teachings on faith only. Literally. This is the phenomena of religion, in all its varying forms. However difficult or shocking the truth is, it has the effect of uniting all of the world's religions by divulging their common origins. Even some of the abductees were encouraged by our otherworldly visitors to write books to try disseminating the truth to those who would listen, and those who are ready to listen. Thanks for that too. They are trying to mitigate the trauma that truth causes.

Do we want to live in blissful ignorance and sweet denial of the truth that we are not alone? How will it affect our daily lives to incorporate this truth in our consciousness? In general, the reason for knowledge is so that it may guide our future actions. We are not after all facing an enemy, who wants to wipe us out and march in to repopulate in our place. They cannot. Some of them evolved in and for life in a different environment. (For example, "gray" extraterrestrial biologic entities cannot be in our direct sunlight.) But they have vision, intelligence and knowledge. One group, which is more human, would have liked us to listen to their offer to abandon nuclear weapons in trade for medical and other knowledge to improve the length and quality of our lives. We did not agree. Another group, which is not so human, said *fine*, keep making nuclear weapons, but allow us to abduct people and use them as resources to change the human genome, to instill some of our genes which enables a telepathic society, where the use of such nuclear weapons is effectively prevented. Like a child with a weapon, we can take away the gun, or help the child to grow wise. Both paths of actions are valid to mitigate risk. In the case of our extraterrestrial guides, the choice was for the later. And the way to make us grow wiser is to instill some of their genetic traits in us. Not all of them – i.e. they are not replacing us *in toto*, but just enough to intervene by physically evolving humanity on Earth. Our improved selves will inherit this promised land. A culture where the individuals have telepathic understanding and influence that links each of them has a natural empathy that balances the ownership of nuclear and other powers. This may be necessary for the continued well-being of our biosphere.

Even if a large portion of our future population is telepathic and genetically enhanced in this way, it may be enough to provide this balance, with the remaining of us linked by an ever-expanding internet and electronically enabled telepathy. Though never as good as the real thing, electrotelepathy will be useful in parallel with working through nature to evolve the cranium. And if we can comprehend all this, then we will understand the importance of the hybridization program undertaken by our extraterrestrial cousins, understand the need for the trauma of the subjects drafted into the program, and how we can mitigate this trauma and the shock to the worldview of the rest of us by integrating these truths into our psyche. After all, the child who grows up is not physically the same any longer. Biological cells and tissues renew. What makes us wonderful intelligent living beings is not necessarily that we are human. Infusion of some helpful alien DNA sequences will not make us scary aliens, any more than the recombination of a father's and mother's genes makes a scary new being. New genes or "new blood" is generally advantageous. Except for identical twins and clones, no two persons are the same. Even then they grow apart as different events influence their lives. So we will be just as wonderful with some alien genes. But then after all, are we not part alien already? Those who study the concept of panspermia know that DNA sequences evolved elsewhere have likely been introduced to Earth before, which largely explains certain gaps in the fossil record – like those of our Homo Sapien ancestry. So this new intervention is not dramatically different than those that have occurred ages ago. What makes it different is that our knowledge and power to destroy has now outpaced our biological and psychosocial capabilities to control it.

Therefore all is good. What is occurring is necessary. There is no need to "shoot down the aliens" just because they seem to fly around our airspace with impunity, since they have the wisdom to control their power and technology, more than we do ours. What is occurring from the larger picture is a "history" which may have already occurred on a different extrasolar planet before, whereat the sequence and timing for a human-like population to grow and attain technology has been recorded. This progression here was therefore foreseen and is the basis of predictions in our Bible.

Chapter 15 – Facts and Hypotheses

It is a fact that the UFO phenomenon is real. It is also a fact that some of these craft are of extraterrestrial origin, and are intelligently controlled. Third, it is a fact that they are clandestinely interacting with a large portion of our population to create hybrid human beings, to include some of their ancestral genetic traits. Fourth, it is a fact that these hybrid (though nearly 100% human) offspring have been integrating into our population with the intention of gaining an increasing proportion. Fifth, it is a fact that both the original alien ancestors and these hybrid offspring have telepathic traits and capabilities which can alter the perception and mental states of a normal human being; in other words, their brain is like a powerful transmitter that can affect the thinking processes in ours.

Hypotheses: It is a hypothesis that the purpose of this alteration and shift in the human genome at this time is because of our level of knowledge and technological achievements. It is also a hypothesis that left to its present course, the growth of human population with its technological luggage will fatally harm this planet's biosphere. Third, it is a hypothesis that there are several extrasolar planets out in this region of our galaxy with populations of intelligent life, some of which are very similar to our own human form. Fourth, it is a hypothesis that some of them have come to visit and intervene in Earth's biosphere in the past, which include interventions in human biology, and cultural intervention in the guise of gods or one powerful God. Fifth, it is a hypothesis that since the age of the dinosaurs was significantly longer on this planet than the age of man, and since other extrasolar planets have similar intelligent populations, then mathematically it follows that there are even more extrasolar planets out there which presently – at this very moment that you are reading my words – have dinosaurs or dinosaur-like large animals living on them. May we one day adventure out there, to other stars and planets and cultures, and experience the journey for our spirit as those who sail the sea.

Chapter 16 – Cosmic Sutra

(a summary in prose)

Origins of Religions

Yahweh was a king of wisdom,
a leader of advanced human beings
from another solar system in this galaxy
who found favor with the obedient Abraham
and guided his descendents Isaac and Israel
to bring forth a culture with moral principles
that would live in harmony with nature.

Yahweh again intervened
three and a half millennia ago
to guide Moses and his people
from the unjust circumstance of slavery
by equally unjust plagues and cruel actions,
then tried again to set moral guidance
with new social laws and commandments.

But his people waned and Yahweh passed,
so with compassion and guidance for others
a new social intervention was planned.
The celestial visitors sent their own son Gabriel
with his seed to bring forth Mary's first child,
and guided him to be a teacher of the spirit
known by many as Jesus, Isa and Jmmanuel.

When Joseph who was betrothed to Mary
first heard of her celestial impregnation
he was filled with anger but was explained
he should become her spouse and help this child
who was destined for a special purpose.
This child then brought a new teaching to others
of love and order and the power of the spirit.

After he was baptized by John in the Jordan
his father Gabriel came to praise him from above,
but the people misunderstood the cosmic source and
eventually thought they had killed him on the cross.
This was not the case and he went on to live
and teach under different names in different lands
including Syria, Turkey, and India where he passed.

Six centuries after the life of Jesus,
Gabriel came down to teach Muhammad
and spread moral guidance to yet another people.
And it was explained here again (Qur'an 4.157)
that they thought they killed the Messiah,
but they did not kill him nor crucify him,
and that it only appeared so to them.

In this way by teaching at first only a chosen few,
then later others across many millennia and lands,
our celestial visitors from a sister solar system
spread their teachings of moral values and laws
and they appeared as if a divine being from above.
But the truth must be known that like in Buddhism
there is only enlightenment for the evolving soul.

Cosmic Travel

For over a century we have known
of Einstein's theory of Special Relativity,
whereby as a traveler approaches the speed of light
his time and aging slows down with dilation of time.
At the speed of light minus one mile per hour,
he can traverse a thousand light years of distance
and age only twenty days in his biological clock.

Although time at his origin and
destination will elapse normally,
and he will traverse a thousand light years
in no less than a thousand years,
his own aging of only twenty days
within dilated time at such high speeds
will easily enable him to make the trip.

In this way advanced intelligent life
has easily come to Earth from afar,
and their knowledge of cosmic history
from other races and civilizations
can only help us develop and evolve.
History repeats itself and the past lessons learned
from other cultures is like the future to us.

Commandments

Celebrate every day but rest and meditate on truth to give
    your life direction
Love and respect your father and mother and all life and
    all things

Do not kill unless you can create life and avoid harming a
    spirit
Do not steal because it is unjust and brings disturbance
    into the mind
Do not commit adultery for overpopulation harms the
    environment
Do not bear false witness and speak an untruth or curse
    the truth
Do not greedily covet your neighbor's wife, wealth or
    possessions

Natural Laws

The natural laws of Creation dwell in all things.
Principles of mathematics and evolution,
And the laws of physics and chemistry,
And the laws of biochemistry which builds life,
And the law of cause and effect that manifests time,
And the law of the mind that like attracts like,
All of which you learn from nature to become wise.

Universal Harmony

Be harmonious with the whole universe,
By giving thanks and gratitude to all that exists.
Thank your brother and sister and father and mother
And all who come in contact with you because
The laws of Creation dwell in all persons and things.
We are all part of an interrelated cosmic symphony,
We are all children and all perfect in grand harmony.

Life of Peace

Go seek out and learn other cultures,
Marry those of other races and places,
And unite the world by eliminating nationalism.
We are all ambassadors of civilization,
Members of a vast sea of consciousness,
Each of us is a fraction of the Creation,
Yet an inseparable part of the universe.

The natural laws and eternal principles
that preexisted and permeate the universe
are within each of us and guide our lives
in an interconnected symphony
and will continue to unfold all that exists
in perfect peace and grand harmony
now and forever more.

Like each molecule of water in a vast sea,
each of our minds and thoughts together
form the vast sea of consciousness,
resulting in waves of ideas
that manifest in the physical world
by our externalized actions.
This is the process of creation.

Left to itself within a closed system,
disorder of matter and entropy always increases.
But when life is added, it is special
because it brings order to matter
to build structure and consciousness.
Life is also special because it can make

copies of itself to duplicate and create.

Meditation

O Vast Universe, which gives life and shelter to all living
    beings,
Fill my whole being with Spirit and a sense of Oneness.
My life is not my own to claim,
It is a fraction of the Creation that permeates the
    universe.
My acts are not my own to claim,
They are the acts of the Creative Process that unfolds the
    universe.
May the spirits that surround and incarnate within us,
    guide us and protect us

I now leave the world
of the five senses
and expand my mind
into the Spiritual Realm.
This is the Great Oneness
that enfolds us
in a vast sea of consciousness.

I visualize Creation's Attributes as a...
Vast Sea of Infinite Wisdom...
Vast Sea of Infinite Love...
Vast Sea of Infinite Life...
Vast Sea of Infinite Abundance...
Vast Sea of Infinite Joy...
Vast Sea of infinite Harmony...

I am in the world of Grand Harmony, and as part of this
    Vast Creation,
I am receiving an infinite supply of infinite life power.
The infinite life power is flowing into me, flowing into me
    (inhale),
The infinite life power is filling me, sustaining me,
filling me, sustaining me, *(hold breath then exhale)*.
Thank you very much! This is no longer my life,
but the life of Grand Oneness of Creation that dwells
    within me.

Prayer for World Peace...
Creation's infinite energy flows into us, and shines forth
    from us
As a brilliant spiritual light of love.
The spiritual light of love grows and grows in intensity,
Covering the entire world,
And filling the hearts of all mankind, with thoughts only
    of Love, Peace,
Order and the Truth of Oneness in a Vast Sea of
    Consciousness.

Prayer

My mind and spirit you exist with omnipotence,
May your nature be holy and held divine,
May your kingdom incarnate itself within me,
May your power unfold itself within me, on Earth and in
    the heavens.
Give me today my daily bread that I may recognize the
    truth,

And lead me not into temptation and delusion but deliver
   me from error.
For yours is the kingdom within me and the power and
   knowledge forever.

The Future

Like with Noah but unlike a flood,
there will be conflagration and calamities.
Like the correction of the stock market,
there will be a correction on the Earth,
because exponential growth of people
and exponential destruction of the biosphere
in our environment can only continue so long.

Don't think this is a bad thing or the end,
because life on this and other worlds
will continue as perfectly as it always has.
This correction is just nature's way
to apply the natural laws and principles
in bringing balance and grand harmony.
Those who are enlightened will survive.

Thereafter this world will go on,
but there will be some changes.
It is clear that all the moral guidance
of the world religions over time
from our brothers in the cosmos
were not sufficient to avert world wars
and the decline of the Earth's biosphere.

Their next intervention is necessary,
which is to change the human genome.
This is happening today and now,
one and a half millennia after Muhammad,
two millennia after Jesus, and
three and a half millennia after Moses,
a new humanity is destined to emerge.

CHAPTER 17 – COSMIC POEM:

Dance of the Black Holes

Oh Moon, Oh Sun, you're both long gone
All life has graduated
The Black Hole at the center of the Milky Way
Has grown until its spirals have dissipated

The last star of the last spiral
Has fallen below the event horizon
And what was once a whole galaxy
Is now collapsed into a tiny volume

Other galaxies fare the same
Their cosmic evolution is complete
Andromeda and the rest
Are but dark masses of gravity

Chemistry is long dead
Since no atoms have survived
But physics is alive and well
With subatomic particles packed so tight

All that remains in the universe
Are great Black Holes
They sail together on waves of gravity
Attracting each other oh so close

Some come to orbit others
And some collide

An exquisite cosmic dance of Black Holes
Zigzags over millennia of time

Eventually they spin closer
And collide more often
Until they all merge
Into one massive dot

The universe has collapsed
Tis the end of a cycle
All the spirits can now
Finally rest and smile

ABOUT THE AUTHOR:

Thomas Joseph Kardos was born in Hungary, shortly after the Hungarian Revolution. He emigrated to the United States in 1969, and came to enjoy the freedoms available in this new country. He spent many hours in the ocean – which was something new, and later spent several years with the Sea Scouts. In 1980 he received his Master of Science degree in electrical engineering and computer science from the University of California at Berkeley, then in 1995-96 completed one year of an M.D./Ph.D. program at the University of Kentucky College of Medicine, and has spent his professional life designing computerized medical devices. In 1999, 2001, 2003 and 2005 he participated in the Newport-Ensenada yacht race. In 2001 he sailed the 35 foot trimaran "Capella" solo to Hawaii, and in 2005 sailed the 35 foot trimaran "Therapy" to Costa Rica and the Galapagos Islands, during which the thoughts for this book were formed. Tom served on the Board of Directors of MUFON Orange County in 2000-2001, and as Vice President of the Seicho-No-Ie Orange County chapter in 2009. He is a Propagator of the Seicho-No-Ie, Peace by Faith movement. He also holds a USCG Masters license and an FAA Commercial Pilot license for airplanes and helicopters.

About the cover:
The Japanese symbols for Jitsu Wu Chu are shown, meaning Truth Universe, or Cosmic Truth, which symbolizes the message in this book. Please send your comments regarding the book to: cosmic.truth@yahoo.com